The Original
My Friend Churchey
And
His Sunken Island of Mu

The Original My Friend Churchey and His Sunken Island of Mu

Author: Percy Tate Griffith (1876 – 1950)
Foreword: Dr. John W. Hoopes
Preface: Jack E. Churchward
Publisher: Jack E. Churchward

My Friend Churchey and His Sunken Island of Mu became public domain in 2020, seventy (70) years after the passing of Percy Tate Griffith (1876 - 1950.)

Published in the United States of America
by Jack E. Churchward

Copyright © 2023 by Jack E. Churchward

All rights reserved. No part of this work may be reproduced, stored in a retrieval system, or transmitted in any form or by any means, electronic, mechanical, photocopying, recording, or otherwise, without the permission of the publisher.

ISBN-13: 978-1-7330566-3-2 (paperback)
ISBN-13: 978-1-7330566-4-9 (ePub)

Contents

Foreword vii
Preface xiii
I. Colonel James Churchward, Engineer, Inventor and Author of the Mu Books 1
II. Boyhood Days and "Churchey" 16
III. Churchward, Le Plongeon, Mu, Razor King Gillette and Some Others 30
IV. Churchey, Spikes, and Tie-Plates, Patents and Me 44
V. The Colonel Helps Me Smash a Gang of Racketeers 58
VI. Colonel Churchward Strays Into the Jungle of Steel 71
VII. I Win $275,000 For My Old Friend Churchey 85
VIII. Adventures in Steel .... Bright Hopes for Churchward 103
IX. I Win Colonel Churchward A Million Dollars 126
X. The Law Giveth and The Law Taketh Away 151
XI. The Navy, Justice, and War Department Play Puss in the Corner With Churchey and Me 169
XII. Senator Coleman Du Pont Intervenes .... President Harding, Secretary Davis and Jesse Smith 183
XIII. Churchey Turns For Solace to Mu and the Mayans 196
XIV. A Sunken Churchey and a Sunken Continent Both Emerge from Undeserved Oblivion 220

Foreword

John W. Hoopes
Department of Anthropology
The University of Kansas

James Churchward was a remarkable, imaginative visionary, one of the great pioneers in the early creation of what has become a staple genre of our times: a narrative presented as history and archaeology when in fact it is a work of imaginative fiction. We have become accustomed to this genre in cable TV such as History® (formerly known as the History Channel) and streaming services such as Netflix. James' series about the lost continent of Mu was the hardcopy antecedent to popular "reality TV" series such as the 1970s *In Search of...* and today's *Ancient Aliens*. Erich von Däniken, when confronted with criticisms of his bestselling book *Chariots of the Gods?* (1986), explained that it fit within a genre of speculative nonfiction that had become popular in Europe at the time. He was probably referring to books such as Louis Pauwels and Jacques Bergier's *Le matin des magiciens* (1960), which had a significant influence on his own. It is one of the ur-texts of today's fringe literature, including conspiracy theories about how archaeologists conspire to conceal the truth about the ancient past. Percy Griffith's *My Friend Churchey and His Sunken Continent* is a part of this history.

In fact, speculative nonfiction was much older, with roots in the treatises of the Theosophical Society that had directly inspired James's books: the massive, two-volume works *Isis Unveiled: A Master-Key to the Mysteries of Ancient and Modern Science and Theology* (1877) and *The Secret Doctrine, the Synthesis of Science, Religion and Philosophy* (1888) by Helena Petrovna Blavatsky. Other early works of speculative nonfiction that had directly inspired him included Ignatius Donnelly's *Atlantis: The Antediluvian World* (1882), William Scott-Elliot's *The Story of Atlantis* (1896) and *The Lost Lemuria* (1904), and Augustus Le Plongeon's *Sacred Mysteries Among the Mayas and the Quiches* (1886) and *Queen M'oo and the Egyptian Sphinx* (1900). The latter were especially influential due to James's personal acquaintance with the Le Plongeons, particularly Alice Dixon Le Plongeon, a Theosophist and author the epic poem *Queen Moo's Talisman: The Fall of the Maya Empire* (1902). According to Griffith's biography, James had discussed both Queen Moo and the continent of Mu with Augustus—who had been the first to refer to it as such—and Alice before the turn of the 20th century. Le Plongeon had been especially inspired by Heinrich Schliemann's identification of a mound in western Turkey as ancient Troy and James was inspired by Heinrich's claimed grandson Paul, who in 1912 published an article in the tabloid *New York American* entitled, "How I Discovered Atlantis, the Source of All Civilization." James, born in 1851, was a generation younger than Le Plongeon, born in 1825, but the two were kindred spirits. The difference was in their seriousness. Le Plongeon's photographs typically show him as grim and stern. James, on the other hand, appears with a flower in his lapel, a pointed goatee, and an unmistakable twinkle in his eye.

I first encountered James' books in 1974, when I was a fifteen-year-old Junior in high school. I had come across them in what was probably the "metaphysical/New Age" section of a bookstore in Baltimore, located just a few miles from Savitria, a commune that had been started by Rosicrucian artist Robert Hieronimus. That summer, I enrolled at the Aquarian University of Maryland (AUM) to take a course in "non-Euclidean geometry" in which we played with compasses and squares and visual takes on perspective and imaginary spaces. I had been a fan of science fiction since grade school and that interest had turned to a taste for Victorian sci-fi classics by H. G. Wells and early fantasy fiction literature, especially work of A. Merritt and H. P. Lovecraft. In fact, I have a distinct memory of buying *The Shuttered Room*, one of the Ballantine paperbacks of Lovecraft's fiction—one with lurid cover art of dripping green face—at the same time I purchased *The Lost Continent of Mu*. The latter was the first in a series of books whose covers had trippy, psychedelic images of women either naked or in flowing robes. The blurb boasted, "Fantastic—but true! The scientific and mystical discovery of a strange civilization that disappeared 50,000 years ago! 'Intensely interesting.'" I later went back and bought all the titles I could find in the same series. I was a voracious reader, a habit I acquired from my mother, an *aficionada* of anything having to do with ancient Egypt. She had been an avid member of AMORC, also known as the Rosicrucian Order, founded by Harvey Spencer Lewis in 1915. Mu was something different, but with similar appeal. At fifteen, the hints of a relationship between James' Muans (a.k.a. Mayans) and ancient Egyptians intrigued me.

When I arrived at Harvard in 1982, the summer before I was to begin a doctoral program in anthropology with a focus on the archaeology of Central America—especially the ancient Mayas—my first job was with a professor with whom I bonded on our familiarity with James and *The Lost Continent of Mu*. In his *Fantastic Archaeology: A Walk on the Wild Side of North American Prehistory* (1991), Stephen Williams, the Peabody Professor of American Archaeology and Ethnology at Harvard, tells the story of how as a teenager he had become "deeply hooked on the mysteries of Mu" due to a fortuitous encounter with James' 1926 book in prep school. It became his entrée into the profession of archaeology. Like me, he had made the shift from pseudoarchaeology (literature that purports to be archaeology but does not follow the rules of that discipline) to academic archaeology before starting college at Yale. However, each of us shared a bemused nostalgia for our indulgences in fantasy and imaginings of lost continents, whether Atlantis in the Atlantic Ocean or Mu (a.k.a. Lemuria) in the Pacific. I was Williams' research assistant for developing a new and ultimately popular undergraduate course at Harvard called "Fantastic Archaeology," in which James's work was on the syllabus as classic example of the topic addressed in its title. The course was one in which Williams taught skills of critical thinking by discussing "fantastic" claims about Stonehenge, Easter Island, the Great Pyramid, lost continents, hyperdiffusionism (ancient transoceanic journeys), and of course von Däniken's ancient astronauts. Williams had a detailed lecture in which he discussed Blavatsky, Donnelly, Le Plongeon, James Churchward and their fantastic ideas about Atlantis and Mu.

The value of James' work for me was that it encouraged me to exercise my imagination. I have long told my students that one of the required skills of a successful archaeologist is the ability to imagine and hold entire worlds in one's head, something akin to what video gamers and fans of role-playing games such as *Dungeons and Dragons* are also adept at doing. That is, in order to do archaeology well, one must be able to provisionally reconstruct what an ancient society would have been like: its people, their food, their artifacts, their buildings, and their beliefs. This is precisely what James did in imaging ancient Mu. However, it is essential to avoid confusing a rich imagination with reality. The territory of Mu, its artwork, and its mysterious Naacal tablets were the products of a rich imagination of the kind encouraged by the Theosophical Society, whose members included L. Frank Baum, author of a fourteen-volume series whose first book was *The Wonderful Wizard of Oz* (1900). However, instead of presenting his imaginary land as fiction—as Baum did with Oz—James asserted Mu was real. James was not the only one in his family who had a fascination with human origins. His brother Albert, one year younger and an active Freemason, had published *Signs & Symbols of Primordial Man: Being an Explanation of the Evolution of Religious Doctrines from the Eschatology of the Ancient Egyptians* (1910), *The Origin and Evolution of Primitive Man* (1912), *The Origin and Evolution of the Human Race* (1920), *The Arcana of Freemasonry* (1922), and *The Origin and Evolution of Religion* (1924). They had probably both avidly read Zelia Nuttall's 1901 tome, published by the Peabody Museum at Harvard, *The Fundamental Principles of Old and New World Civilizations: A Comparative Research Based on a Study of the Ancient Mexican Religious, Sociological and Calendrical Systems*. They may also have read Madison Grant's notorious book, *The Passing of the Great Race: or, The Racial Basis of European History*. However, despite their shared fascination with the origins of humanity and especially religion, the brothers appear to have had radically different perspectives on the ancient past and the origins of civilization. Albert never mentioned Mu.

First appearing in 1926, a year after Albert's death, James' *The Lost Continent of Mu* fulfilled a desire for non-academic readers to learn more about ancient civilizations, even ones that were not real. Four years earlier, in 1922, Howard Carter had opened the tomb of Tutankhamen, sparking a popular fascination with ancient Egypt, whose place in the Bible was well-known but whose historical details remained esoteric to non-Egyptologists. However, in the 1920s the archaeology of South Asia, Southeast Asia, Indonesia, and the Pacific Islands was in its infancy. There were fascinating hints of what was to be found. For example, in 1915 archaeologist Katharine Routledge and her husband William undertook the first archaeological expedition to Rapa Nui (Easter Island), identifying and excavating some of the famous moai, or monumental statues. Routledge published the expedition's results in *The Mystery of Easter Island* (1919), a book that sparked the imagination of armchair explorers around the world, including James and Lovecraft, who would later incorporate the mysterious ruins into their writings about the fictional places Mu and R'lyeh, represented as nonfiction and fiction, respectively.

The 1920s were a peak period for the Theosophical Society, whose international headquarters in Adyar, India became the center of a Western fascination with Eastern religions. Under the leadership of Annie Besant, the successor to Blavatsky, the society surged in membership. Its success paralleled that of the Indian National Congress, an anti-colonialist, anti-Christian, Hindu and Buddhist revival movement of which Besant—concurrent with her

leadership of the Theosophical Society, which had begun in 1907—became the first president in 1917. One of the preoccupations of the Theosophical Society at the time was the promotion of young Jiddhu Krishnamurthi, a youth from India who had been groomed by Besant, Charles Webster Leadbeater, and other society members to be the Maitreya, a spiritual "World Teacher." In May 1925, Theosophical Society member and South America explorer Colonel Percy Fawcett set out to find a lost civilization in the heart of the Amazon rain forest—an expedition touted by the *Los Angeles Times* with the headline "Explorers enter jungles to seek lost white race"— but never returned. James's first book, *The Lost Continent of Mu, the Motherland of Men* (1926) was published during this heady time and found a ready audience among Society members, who were already familiar with Lemuria through the work of Blavatsky and Scott-Elliot, and also Col. Fawcett's avid supporters. However, in 1929, before the publication of *The Children of Mu* (1931), the second book in the series, Krishnamurthi renounced his anticipated crowning as a New Age messiah, asserting, "truth is a pathless land, and you cannot approach it by any path whatsoever, by any religion, by any sect."
Another noteworthy event that followed the *The Lost Continent of Mu* was the publication of Manly Palmer Hall's *magnum opus*, *The Secret Teaching of All Ages* subtitled *An Encyclopedia Outline of Masonic, Hermetic, Qabbalistic and Rosicrucian Symbolical Philosophy* (1928), which cited Albert's work but not James'. Completed when the author was only twenty-seven years old and sold by subscription, this large and weighty tome assembled a wealth of esoterica. Other noteworthy occult writers of the 1920s included Rudolf Steiner— who had left Theosophy to form Anthroposophy, and the White Russian artist and explorer Nicholas Roerich, who led a high-profile, real-life expedition to Tibet and Central Asia from 1925 to 1929 and whose paintings of Himalayan fastnesses inspired the verbal imagery of H. P. Lovecraft. In 1928, two years after the appearance of *The Lost Continent of Mu*, Lovecraft published his short story "The Call of Cthulhu." It quickly became a classic tale of manuscripts found, horrifying nightmares, and the release of a vengeful, tentacled Old One from his ancient resting place on an island in the Pacific—which for many may have seemed like the peak of one of the sunken mountains of Mu.

The Great Depression began in 1929 (unrelated to but after Krishnamurthi's renunciation) and readers were drawn to James's books about Mu the way they were drawn to *The Wizard of Oz* (1939), Busby Berkeley musicals, and Shirley Temple. His fantasies offered people with limited college education a sense of erudition and an "insider's" glimpse into what they were led to believe were the origins of the mysterious Orient. Novels such as James Hilton's *Lost Horizon* (1933) and the Academy Award winning 1937 film based on it directed by Frank Capra, offered the story of the lost Shangri La and its hidden Himalayan valley of immortality. James published three additional books in his series: *The Sacred Symbols of Mu* (1933), *Cosmic Forces of Mu* (1934), and *Second Book of the Cosmic Forces of Mu* (1935). The Depression was a boon for archaeology in the U.S. with FDR's Works Projects Administration (WPA) hiring hundreds of unskilled laborers to help archaeologists unearth features and artifacts across the country. It is worth noting that popular fascination with what we can now recognize as pseudoarchaeology was a factor in the creation of the Society for American Archaeology, first chartered in 1935 as a professional organization dedicated to promoting and upholding high standards of scholarship—exactly the opposite of what James's books and other similar fantasies represented. This was academic gatekeeping, undertaken in response to runaway "speculative nonfiction." It is probably fair to say that James played a role, albeit indirect, in the creation of what is now the world's largest professional association of archaeologists, both vocational and non-vocational. However, he died the following year, and never witnessed the consequences. Thankfully, he also missed dinosaur-riding comic-book cave man Alley Oop as a resident of his lost continent, as chronicled in *Alley Oop in The Invasion of Moo* (1935) and the 1938 issues *Alley Oop and Dinny in the Jungles of Moo*, *Alley Oop and the Missing King of Moo*, and *Alley Oop and the Cave Men of Moo*.

In the 1950s, James's books attracted the interest of post-WWII dabblers in esoterica, among them writer William S. Burroughs of the Beats, a one-time aspiring archaeologist who was fascinated by ancient mysteries as well as pulp fiction. However, it wasn't until the 1960s, with the release of Churchward's books in inexpensive paperback editions, that interest in the lost land of Mu was revived. In the 1970s, one of James's own illustrations from *The Lost Continent of Mu*, of a seven-headed cobra identified as a Naga, was adopted as the emblem of the Symbionese Liberation Army, a radical, militant organization that undertook various acts of terrorism between 1973 and 1975, including the kidnapping and brainwashing of heiress Patricia Hearst. One can only imagine that the popular paperback editions of his books were popular items in counterculture and prison libraries.

In 1987, I completed my dissertation in archaeology under the direction of Gordon Willey, one of the founding members of the Society for American Archeology in 1935, and embarked upon an academic career. I have continued to teach a course called "Archaeological Myths and Realities," a title I inherited from my predecessor Robert J. Squier at the University of Kansas, in which I perpetuate the goals of Stephen Williams' "Fantastic Archaeology." This course brings me back over and over again to the subject of lost continents. I discuss the significance of James's books about the lost continent of Mu, pointing out that the inclusion of rich detail is not an indication of scientific rigor and that the emotional appeal of lost worlds can contribute to logical fallacies in wishful thinking. I encourage students to dig into the archaeology of these imaginary worlds, learning about James and other authors of his ilk. I hope *My Friend Churchey* will be one of the books they consider.

There never was a lost continent of Mu anywhere but in the imagination of James and his readers. The science of plate tectonics, which found widespread acceptance among geologists in 1968, demonstrated that continents do not rise and sink, but slowly slide around on a sphere of molten magma. The mysterious Naacal tablets and the oddly incised stones of William Niven were fantasies and hoaxes with no archaeological reality. The fieldwork of Sir Mortimer Wheeler in the 1940s revealed an ancient civilization in the Indus Valley, but no sign of Mu.

However, just as the unreal fictions of "reality TV" appeal to wide audiences, the imagined reality of Mu will persist. It has entered into the realm of counterculture and New Age folklore in a fashion that is no easier to shake than speculative nonfiction about aliens and UFOs. Although Mu is not real, at least not with respect to the ancient history of the Earth and humankind, it is an example of the kinds of narratives, from the Bible to Oz to Middle Earth and the Marvel Universe, that invite readers to entertain realities other than the ones that scientists explore. Sometimes these thoughts are enhanced through the use of cannabis, magic mushrooms, or other potent psychedelics. Sometimes they benefit from meditation and visualization. These realities may well exist in parallel universes. Who is to say that they don't?

Preface

Jack E. Churchward

I received a copy of the typewritten pages identified as the unpublished *My Friend Churchy and His Sunken Island of Mu* in the late 1990s. I was contacted via email by Joan Griffith (1932 – 2011) and when we spoke on the telephone, she invited me to visit her home about an hour away in central Florida. Having worked for the Association for Research and Enlightenment for many years in Virginia Beach, Virginia and an ardent believer in the theories of James Churchward, she wished to connect with a member of the family. I visited her home on a Saturday afternoon bringing along the complimentary copy of *Books of the Golden Age* I had received from the publisher. The publisher, Brotherhood of Life, had included the book with my purchase of some of James' scrapbooks and photos. After normal pleasantries, our discussion turned to what I knew about James' life history. I related the story my father told me; James made up his books on his misinterpretation of a Bible passage. James' legal wife, Mary Julia (nee Stephens,) lived six months a year in the same home as my father and "that scoundrel's name was not to be mentioned when she was present." I knew very little about James and never took the opportunity to read his books. Joan took out a sheet of paper and mentioned she had hired the services of a private investigator to look into James' background.

The information on the sheet of paper piqued my interest as I had read correspondence from the "Mary Julia" faction, but I had yet to take a close look at the contents of the scrapbooks or much information from the "James" faction. She then brought out a xeroxed copy of the original manuscript of *My Friend Churchey*… Written by Percy Tate Griffith (1876 – 1950) after James Churchward's death, the manuscript was passed to Joan, his daughter. She described the pages as the 'complete text,' noting Peter Tompkins in his book *Secrets of the Mexican Pyramids* had mentioned only six of the original fourteen chapters had survived.[1] This copy had all fourteen chapters and Ms. Griffith explained the missing pages appeared on top of some boxes after a family move. In return, I gave Joan my copy of *Books of the Golden Age*.

Our agreement was I would only publish the table of contents and first chapter on the webpages I had recently started, allowing her to rewrite the manuscript to bring the language up to that recognizable to modern audiences. Any public release of the original manuscript would wait until after the publication of her book so as not to interfere with her sales. Joan's belief in James' theories was complete and she mentioned, as a small child, she had met James. He had slipped her a small slip of paper at their last meeting urging her to continue the research.[2] Joan also mentioned how ironic it was she lived on Darwin Street. I continued building a small private website to collect facts. The investigator's background notes on James provided the start to build a timeline and opened many avenues of research into my great-grandfather. I heard from Joan twice more, once she provided a Word copy (on a floppy disk)

---

[1] Tompkins, Peter; *Mysteries of the Mexican Pyramids*; Harper & Roe Publishers; 1976; page 365
[2] James passed away in 1936, meaning Joan Griffith would have been at most, four years old when she received her gift from the "Colonel."

of her version of James' biography and another time to talk about a scandal over unreported deaths during a hurricane. I did not open her manuscript as she was upset I had posted the table of contents on a website. She felt constrained as to the content she could write due to the existing chapter titles. I knew her work had an obvious bias and would repeat only the information supporting James' theories.

In 2006, I was contacted by Dick Laudermilk from South Carolina, and he requested a meeting. My wife and I with Mr. Laudermilk had lunch at the Belleview Biltmore Hotel in Bellaire, Florida and recorded a brief podcast.[3] He purchased the rights to the rewritten *My Friend Churchey…* and published it.[4]

From the original manuscript, clearly Percy Tate Griffith (PTG) knew and interacted with James, although there was a great age difference between the two men. James was in his 40s in the 1890s when Percy writes about the Sunday afternoon talks at his parents' home as a teenager. PTG remarks that others joined in these Sunday afternoon parlor talks, including Augustus Le Plongeon and his wife Alice, as well as "people with a thirst for learning, devotees of the fine arts, poets, musicians, thinkers."[5]

Griffith's complete acceptance of the elder Churchward's illustrious background was a mistake. Adequate documentation exists to support a different picture of James' life before meeting Percy. On the other hand, Griffith's description of events where he was personally involved should be accepted at face value. When Percy acted as James' attorney or otherwise engaged in activities together, I cannot but trust the first-hand account elaborated by Griffith in the manuscript. As for the different picture of James, the following is presented:

James' concocted persona of being a Colonel in the Bengal Lancers and a graduate of Royal Military College, Sandhurst (RMC) and Oxford University are fiction. Communications with the latter two institutions have failed to demonstrate his matriculation at either place of higher learning. The same was true of his so-called military service.

James was born in 1851 in Bridestowe, Devonshire, England. Census documents show James, with his older brother John, was employed as a Banker's clerk in 1871 and living at 7 Cambridge Road, Croydon, London, England. The same entry shows his younger brother Albert as a medical student, later a noted surgeon and author. Also, a marriage certificate from the 18th of December 1871 shows James (with profession of Clerk) marrying Mary Julia Stephens in Kensington. The January 24th, 1872 edition of the *Overland Ceylon Observer and Fortnightly Summary of Intelligence*" recorded Mr. and Mrs. Churchward arriving in Ceylon (Sri Lanka) on the P and O Delhi from England. The same newspaper shows the birth of a son in October 1872 and James' subsequent exploits as a Tea Planter through 1881.[6]

---

[3] Interview with Dick Lawdermilk (Publisher of James' Bio (audio only); 2006
[4] Griffith, Joan T.; *My Friend Churchey and His Sunken Island of Mu: Biography of Colonel James Churchward Engineer, Inventor and Author of the Mu Books*; Ancient Mysteries Press; 2004
[5] Griffith, Percy Tate; *My Friend Churchey and His Sunken Island of Mu*; 1937; page 31
[6] *More James Churchward, Tea Planter*; My-mu.com blog; https://web.archive.org/web/20160402004435/http://blog.my-mu.com/?p=2296; 2016

Additionally, I am in possession of family correspondence from James' lawful wife Mary Julia to James' older brother William Gould Churchward (who was also present as a witness at their 1871 marriage.) The letter indicates she had listened to James' tall tales on WNYC radio from New York. She disputes the fact he ever served in a regular military unit. She also remarked she had heard him retell a story the two of them listened to on one of their voyages from Ceylon (now Sri Lanka.)

Despite his statements in his books (or exaggerations to friends) concerning his military service and education, James was a London banker's clerk turned tea planter in Sri Lanka and not a senior military officer or graduate of an institute of higher learning.

James' story of Mu, beginning with the 1926, *Lost Continent of Mu Motherland of Man*, was based on the purported translation of tablets he had discovered while he was on alleged famine relief duty in India in the British military. In his books, James called them the Naacal tablets and claimed they were the records of an ancient, advanced civilization. Forty years after his earth-changing discovery he brought the once-secret knowledge to print. Nobody had ever heard of these tablets before, or had they?

James' first book about Mu was not the first mention of tablets. The November 10, 1924 edition of the *New York American* reports 125 (unnamed) tablets found by 'Colonel' Churchward and translated by Buddhist scholars were soon to be made public. In January 1925, articles appearing under the title "Cradle of the Human Race?" and "Flying Machines 10,000 B.C." appeared in the press mentioning the theories of Lieutenant-Colonel James Churchward with his 125 tablets and Buddhist scholars.[7] These were syndicated articles with a wide distribution in newspapers across the world.

The version related in James' books assert the tablets were shown to James by a Rishi in a temple in India after becoming friends over a period of years. The commute from Sri Lanka must have been horrendous and he had to juggle all those chores to oversee on the plantation. The Rishi also taught him the ancient Naacal language to translate the tablets. Gone from the newest version were the number of tablets and the assistance of the Buddhist scholars (and he got a promotion to Colonel.) As shown in *My Friend Churchey...* James invented the Naacal tablets to use in a fictional romance story.[8] He admits to Percy he named his tablets after an entry he found in 'one of Le Plongeon's books.'[9] [10] Augustus Le Plongeon identifies the term in *Queen Moo and the Egyptian Sphinx* as:

---

[7] *Naacal Tablets – Further Data Revealed*; My-Mu.com blog; https://web.archive.org/web/20141204210742/http://blog.my-mu.com/?p=1680; 2014
[8] Griffith, Percy Tate; *My Friend Churchey and His Sunken Island of Mu*; 1937; page 210
[9] Ibid, pages 206-207
[10] The Foundation for the Advancement of Mesoamerican Studies, Inc on their webpages, "A Grammar of the Yucatecan Mayan Language" provides the following description:
"Naac is the verb root for indicating upward motion. As noted in the transitive conjugation naac appears with the causative marker particle -z- placed between it and the verbal suffixes. The meaning of the verb in the transitive conjugation is "to lift". In the intransitive conjugation however the meaning of naacal is "to climb, to raise up".
"A Grammar of the Yucatecan Mayan Language; Foundation for the Advancement of Mesoamerican Studies, Inc.; https://web.archive.org/web/20210117040039/http://www.famsi.org/reports/96072/grammar/section14.htm

Mayan adepts, known as the Naacal (Naacal = 'the Exalted') traveled across the globe colonizing the planet and bringing ancient wisdom and knowledge as Mayan missionaries.[11]

In the 1926 *Lost Continent of Mu Motherland of Men*, his first published book on the subject, James states the following as one of the proofs for his theory:

VALMIKI. *Ramayana*. Vol. I Page 342. — "The Maya adepts, the Naacals, starting from *the land of their birth in the east*, as missionaries of religion and learning went first to Burma and there taught the Nagas. From Burma they went to the Deccan in India, whence they carried their religion and learning to Babylonia and to Egypt."[12]

This passage illustrates one point made by PTG in the manuscript concerning James' plagiarism of Le Plongeon's work. Nearly every descriptor used by Le Plongeon to describe his Naacal is echoed in James' books, except Le Plongeon's Maya went to the east and Churchward's went to the west. My book, "*Lifting the Veil on the Lost Continent of Mu Motherland of Men*," contains further examples.[13]

Additionally, the passage quoted above creates a dichotomy. If the Naacal were the brotherhood of the keepers of ancient wisdom of Mu and all humans were from Mu, where did these other people come from? Why did they require the reintroduction of the Motherland's religion? How and why were these new peoples disconnected from the Motherland? Surely, people from Mu were intelligent enough to bring the necessary infrastructure for their comfort and well-being. It wasn't like the people of Mu didn't have flying machines; James found records of flights lasting from 1000 to 3000 miles.[14]

While *My Friend Churchey and His Sunken Island of Mu* doesn't present detailed information on the daily life of James Churchward and answer every question, it does provide conclusive evidence the Naacal tablets are fictional. James' discovery and alleged translation of the Naacal tablets constructs the foundation of James' narrative and is a fable from the beginning. Without the Naacal tablets, there is no link between the other "evidence" he cites to create a now sunken continent in the Pacific Ocean. His theories are built on a non-existent foundation.

I have no response to those who may criticize this work. Three years into the public domain, the information contained herein provides a more complete picture of my great-grandfather, James Churchward; one of the goals I set when I started my research. Prior to starting my part-time research in 2005, I had to rely on what my father told me about his books and the theories therein. I could parrot – it is all nonsense, or actually engage in a study of his life and works to come to my own conclusion. The astute reader will recognize I have had the

---
[11] LePlongeon, Augustus; *Queen Moo and the Egyptian Sphinx*; 1896; pages xxiii - xxiv
[12] Churchward, James; *The Lost Continent of Mu Motherland of Men*; 1926; page 59
[13] Churchward, Jack; *Lifting the Veil on the Lost Continent of Mu Motherland of Mankind*; 2013
[14] Churchward, James; *Children of Mu*; 1931; page 193

proof all along with a copy of the original *My Friend Churchey...*, however, on the possibility Percy Tate Griffith was somehow biased against James, I still investigated his works and requested comments and feedback. There is and was no smoking gun to prove James' theories correct, no matter what 'evidence' is presented. James' theories do not pass critical examination either. Fantastic theories require fantastic evidence and James' works do not measure up to the task. In my examination of his sources for the 1926 *Lost Continent of Mu Motherland of Men*, I discovered most of his "quotes" were amended to fit his narrative. Many of his proofs are unidentifiable legends, edited quotes from other books, and doctored theories from yellow journalism articles. Layered on top of this "evidence" are the "proofs" from his interpretations of the Naacal tablets that do not exist, except as literary device in a fictional story.

If there is anything correct in James' works, it is that we are all one big human family. I believe there is enough proof to assert we all have a common ancestor, despite cultural and physical differences. James places mankind's birthplace on his now-sunken continent of Mu for one very special reason. According to his works, the Supreme Creator put humans there hundreds of thousands of years ago and then all the evidence of His workings were eliminated. These circumstances provide a mechanism to disprove evolution. Understanding James postulates the Christian Bible is a mistranslation of the Naacal tablets passed down to Moses (a Naacal adept) brings a metaphysical tone and moral authority to allow the existence of a Supreme Creator instead of "being descended from apes." James refused, as many people did at the time, to accept a non-heavenly origin for humanity. James writes the "Neanderthal, Piltdown, and Heidelberg man" discoveries "were those of idiots and degenerates is obvious from the abnormal shapes of their skulls." and outcasts shunned by civilization.[15] Although there may be agreement on the overall conclusion of being one big happy family, the route taken to arrive at that point can be disputed. When, as a collective we, realize the possibility of one big happy family, perhaps we can find enough common ground to live in peace and harmony.

In my research, I am occasionally confronted with accusations the works of James Churchward were racist. While James' theories do rob indigenous peoples of their hard-won accomplishments, I found no overtly racist content in his works. At no point in his works are any people singled out for being less-than-human; however, obviously his predisposition to believe in the superiority of his culture does introduce elements some might find objectionable. The majority of people I have spoken with point to the hopeful message underlying his works. That message being a possible world where everyone is at peace and harmony. Also, the thoughts and attitudes of anyone born in 1851 can hardly be judged by today's standards. Even the attitudes of those born in the 1950s are today considered barbaric by some people, so it is safe to assume there will be someone to put in their two cents. All that being said, it is all water under the bridge.

---

[15] Churchward, James; *Lost Continent of Mu Motherland of Men*; 1926; page 171

Griffith does inject his dismissal of James' writing ability.[16] Obviously, Percy was unaware of James' earlier writings. Along with brochures for fishing trips on the railroads[17] [18], he also made submissions to Field and Stream magazine where he also wrote a fictional story written under his own name and printed in Recreation magazine in March 1895.[19]

Jack E. Churchward
Clearwater, Florida
July 30, 2023

---

[16] Griffith, Percy Tate; *My Friend Churchey and His Sunken Island of Mu*; 1937; page 200
[17] Churchward, James; *A Big Game and Fishing Guide to North-Eastern Maine*; 1898; https://books.google.com/books?id=mVraXHIFhgEC&printsec=titlepage&hl=en#v=onepage&q&f=false
[18] Churchward, James, *Fishing Among the Thousand Islands*; 1894; https://web.archive.org/web/20130510102128/http://www.my-mu.com/pdf/FishingAmongThousandIslands.pdf
[19] Churchward, James; *Indian Joe. – A Tale of the Thousand Islands*; Recreation; Vol. 2 No.3; March 1895

About 63,000 words

MY FRIEND CHURCHEY

AND HIS

SUNKEN ISLAND OF MU

by

Percy Tate Griffith

CONTENTS

I. Colonel James Churchward, Engineer, Inventor and Author of the Mu Books.

II. Boyhood Days and "Churchey".

III. Churchward, Le Plongeon, Mu, Razor King Gillette and Some Others.

IV. Churchey, Spikes and Tie-Plates, Patents and Me.

V. The Colonel Helps Me Smash A Gang of Racketeers.

VI. Colonel Churchward Strays Into The Jungle of Steel.

VII. I Win $275,000 For My Old Friend Churchey.

VIII. Adventures in Steel .... Bright Hopes for Churchward.

IX. I Win Colonel Churchward A Million Dollars.

X. The Law Giveth and The Law Taketh Away.

XI. The Navy, Justice, and War Departments Play Puss In The Corner With Churchey and Me.

XII. Senator Coleman Du Pont Intervenes.....President Harding, Secretary Davis and Jesse Smith.

XIII. Churchey Turns For Solace To Mu and the Mayans.

XIV. A Sunken Churchey and a Sunken Continent Both Emerge from Undeserved Oblivion.

I.

COLONEL JAMES CHURCHWARD, ENGINEER, INVENTOR AND AUTHOR OF

THE MU BOOKS

IN THE YEAR 1926 there cometed upon the literary and scientific horizon of America and the whole English-speaking world, at a point where the terra firma of factual research meets the unbounded skies of speculative romance, a unique volume entitled The Lost Continent of Mu.

It was from the pen of an Englishman, long resident in the United States, Colonel James Churchward.

Soldier, scholar, student, thinker, explorer, artist, inventor, engineer, metallurgist, expert angler, Mason, he was as well-known in many sections of the country and walks of life, as he was unknown in literature.

He was intermittently in touch with thousands of men in Europe and in remote parts of the world. He was intimately acquainted with innumerable persons, high and low, in the railroad and railway supply field. Wherever fishermen congregated to win and whisk the finny fighters from the waters of America, he was known as an authority and a success. In scientific circles he was a frequent contactor with the metallurgical leaders and the workers in geology and biology, without ever being regarded as orthodox and one of them. As a Mason, he was known in almost every quarter of the globe, as one who had made a study not only of the secrets and science and details of Masonry itself, but also of external facts throwing light on its origins and connections with early tribes of mankind, and with the dominant races during its existence.

He was the discoverer and patentee of the famous Churchward Steel, known in the trade as N C V steel, and in the steel industry was a well-publicized figure, viewed with respect by many, and with bitter hostility and pronounced scepticism and antagonism by others.

I had known him intimately from my earliest boyhood. Been his confidant and adviser in many affairs, as he in my youth had been to me. Had aided him, in his keen and disheartening struggles, his poverty and disasters.

I made him one fortune in Steel and nearly another. Brought his Steel from obscurity to fame and big money, the only money, by the way, he ever made from it, except through the sale of stock in his companies to friends who believed in his genius and his promises.

    We fought side by side in one of the biggest and strangest Patent wars of the century, of all time; winning at Austerlitz, and losing in a Waterloo that was once won but ignobly turned at the end by the ruthlessness of an imperfect judicial system, coupled with the invincible power of Steel and High Finance.

    All the years of our friendship he discussed with me this matter of the sunken continent of Mu. Indeed, I was the means of his first interesting himself in a life-study of it. Though let me enter at once a full disclaimer of any part or suggestion in his works, in his researches on Mu, his conclusions. The same holds true as to his many inventions, his Steel alloy. In all these things, sole credit belongs to himself, for whatever he did or contributed to any of his avenues of expression.

    The Lost Continent of Mu made an instant sensation. It was reviewed widely, featured in Sunday magazine sections. It aroused considerable discussion both in literary and scientific circles.

    The predominant trend of the criticisms was from the outset sceptical. It was recognized that some valuable matter was contained in the Colonel's well-filled volume, but doubt was freely expressed as to much of it.

    This book was followed in 1931 by a similar work, The Children of Mu. In 1933, another, The Sacred Symbols of Mu. In 1934, Cosmic Forces As They Were Taught in Mu.

The thesis and disclosure in these several books was, in a nutshell, that long prior to any of our historically known civilizations, there existed in the South Pacific Ocean a vast continental island, called Mu. The pronunciation of this word, in true Mayan usage, by the way, is Moo. This land was peopled by a race of rather over-intelligent beings, supermen, rendered so by some 200,000 years' progress in culture.

These men and women spread out over the world to colonize and establish the races, dynasties and cultures of Egypt, Greece, Chaldea, India, Persia, The Mayan Yucatan, the land of Atlantis, celebrated by Plato, believed mythical by many scholars, but placed in actual existence by numbers of researchers, some of whom followed the sunken island idea, and others dismissed this catastrophic theory and found evidences of Atlantean nature in various sections of the ancient world.

Mu, according to Colonel Churchward, included practically all Oceania. Most of the thousands of islands of the Pacific Ocean today were in the dim past mountain peaks of Mu. All these islands were continuously connected to form part of the great continent Mu. They all shared the common flora and fauna, people and culture of that vast Mu, and with the rest of the broad lands which encompassed them, were under a single Government and subject to a single religion.

Just as all present civilized races, and all those of historical antiquity, were descended from the people of Mu, so all the arts and crafts, sciences, all religions, all cosmogonies, traditions, legends, folk-lore, customs, superstitions, languages, were derived from those of Mu. Except, of course, those subordinate features obviously arising from a subsequent period of the colonized nation's existence and exigencies.

This Continent of Mu was engulfed in the Pacific by a convulsion of Nature, an earthquake both subterranean and sub-aqueous. All or most of its people, who had not already emigrated to their adopted countries, were annihilated, and were, with their homes, industrial and agricultural and architectural achievements, sunk under the waters of the Pacific, with no traces other than those collected and published by the author.

Veritable masses of evidences and data bearing upon this theory or discovery were marshalled by Colonel Churchward in his works, and regimented there like phalanxes of militant Macedonians. The volumes were colorfully enriched by elaborate and numerous sketches, drawings and paintings of the author, by photostats and photographs of existing fragments of stone, Mss, of allegedly probative matters.

But the foundation of the whole work was the unqualified statement by Colonel Churchward that during his years of sojourn in India with his command, and later, he had been given access by priests to tablets alike sacred and secret, whereon, in a language known to noone else, other than the priests who taught it to the Colonel, were inscribed all the details and minutiae of the topography, climate, ethnology, civilization, manners, religion, history and eventual fate of the Muans or Mayans, as faithfully depicted in the Churchward volumes.

The failure of Colonel Churchward to submit the tablets of the copies of the original inscriptions, to scientists generally, to philologists, archaeologists, antiquarians, with a lexicon of the language which professedly he could himself read, created an unfavorable impression upon such classes, and upon reviewers, and his works were relegated by scholars to the category and Coventry of hybrid fiction and pseudo-science.

Reputedly hundreds of thousands of his books were sold. Certainly many hundreds of thousands believed in him and his disclosures. Thousands of fan letters came to him from all over the country, and from distant corners of the earth. Many contributed relevant and salient facts and statements bolstering up his contentions, which strengthened his case greatly. Tourists, students, researchers, men and women of affairs, came to visit him, overwhelmed him with invitations to their homes, and with hearty welcomes when he came.

Mostly they were believers and disciples, but they were far from being shallow or moronic. Many were serious thinkers, that really high order of humanity who thrill with new knowledge of their ancestral past or predictable future. Fifty years ago Camille Flammarion the eminent French astronomer, cosmologist, naturalist and novelist, estimated there were but fifteen thousand persons in the whole world of two billions, actively interested in seeking out the secrets of their origin, existence and abode here; if ever true, which is doubtful, it is not so in this or recent decades.

Right or wrong, true or false, the thesis of Colonel Churchward was never disproved. His collated evidences were at least a mighty army in support of his arguments. If Time does not show proof of his conclusions, the matter of his works does contain and display many resemblances and relations, parallels, many features and factors of past and present civilizations, both interesting and enlightening, valuable to the student of archaeology, ethnology and history.

When these works were published, and a torrent of reviews and criticisms questioned the discoveries and disclosures of Colonel Churchward, I was approached by many who knew my long years of close association with the author in Steel, and asked about the authenticity of the subject matter.

To all of these I declined to express any opinion, to range myself either in defense or in opposition. I promised that I would at a later date make a statement on Mu, after I had time to devote to it. I was aware that there were elements in the question on which I held information, and that sooner or later it would devolve upon me to disclose them because of my intimate position in the Mu subject, as will hereafter more fully appear.

I knew it would require considerable study of a vast amount of matter, also that there were circumstances which made it difficult for me to make any announcement of my position. Fortunately I occupy no post or altitude of instruction or authority in archaeology necessitating my speaking then, and at least not until the right time to present the facts publicly.

Meanwhile I replied to all, what I can still say today, that I had been familiar with Colonel Churchward's study of Mu, and that in this affair, as in all or most of his other inventions or discoveries, he always had a factual basis, at least, for even his often incredibly radical opinions, dicta, and claims.

How much of all the collocation of details and data, pictures, historical references, and the foundations and superstructure of his bold narrative and fluent description of Mu, its origin, and his own researches, had any valid basis of fact? And what manner of man was he, the author, the claimant of knowledge on this ancient and lost race and continent ? Was he honest, dependable, of good judgment, worthy of credence? Were his motives actually or probably those of the lover of pure science and truth for itself alone?

Rightly to appraise this, besides tracing the pedigrees and weight of his allegations and quotations, one needs to know the man himself, his nature and life-history, how he came to be interested in this subject, and what he personally did and said in connection with it. Not only is it desirable to sift the various elements of his statements and conclusions, but to ascertain how he came to make them, what was his introduction to Mu, what were the steps by which he was led to the ultimate form of his Mu volumes. To analyse the mode of operation of his mind, to know how he thought and spoke in other matters, and how he acted in them.

To understand, in addition, what were the forces of environment working upon him, what strains and stresses had been laid upon him. The impelling and compelling external factors of life which motivated him, which directed him in both the study of Mu and the writing it in the form and details in which it appeared.

In all these connections, it has been my lot to be so informed and so in contact with him, and so directly in touch with this matter of Mu and the Mayans, that I can, within the limits of my powers to convey thought or description, satisfy the requirements;uniquely, in respect to the matters known to me and doubtless not to any other.

The recent death of Colonel Churchward not only has revived speculation and inquiry upon this subject, but frees me to speak fully and with propriety upon it, especially since what I have to submit will be of distinct advantage to his memory, rather than otherwise.

In any case, it is clearly in order that the records of science and literature be given all the facts. This is unquestionably a paramount imperative to which I may not be indifferent. Facts biographical of the life of this unusual genius Churchward. Facts of the great Steel he invented, which should not remain hidden, because of their far-reaching effect upon the world's judgment of that Steel, and of the system by which it was detached from its field of useful service to industry and to the United States military and naval defenses. Facts of his share in the Mu matter, and a complete exposition and answer to all the questions posed regarding the Lost Continent.

And this before those facts change from the status of known to one, to that of known to none . The ability to make a definite and thorough clarification of these matters carries with it the duty to do so. The more so because it will concomitantly do no harm to Colonel Churchward's deserved place in them, but positively do such justice to him in other respects, as far to outweigh any corrections I may make in the matter of the Lost Continent of Mu.

My Friend Churchward and his Sunken Island of Mu

There are two required illustrations, one a "Cosmic Diagram" attached next page 210; the other a sketch map showing location of Mu and Atlantis, opp. page 195 —

If desired to have other illustrations, I have three fishing pictures done by Colonel Churchward, to go in first part of book; and some dozen pages in color of Egyptian Gods copied by Colonel Churchward and given to me, which can be printed in black and white or color, as desired, in various parts of book. One used as frontispiece, a few or all of others distributed.

These available illustrations may be seen at any time.

According to Colonel Churchward, all Egyptian Gods originated in Mu.

These Egyptian pictures, reduced, could be used as Chapter-heading illustrations.

Photo-copies of some Yucatan sculptures from Le Plongeon can also be used; or any other copies or cuts of Yucatan fragments easily obtainable elsewhere.

Pencil sketch of illustration to be supplied.

to face page 210 of Ms.

Illus. for My Friend Churchward and His Sunken Island of Mu.

Pencil. sketch of illustration to be supplied to face page 195 of Ms

Location of Atlantis as placed by Le Plongeon and Churchward; and of Mu in the Pacific as placed by Churchward.

II.

BOYHOOD DAYS AND "CHURCHEY"

I FIRST MET COLONEL JAMES CHURCHWARD when I was so small a boy that I cannot recall just what age I was the day I recognized him as a man and a friend. He was to me, from the outset, a striking and attractive figure in the world about me.

He was an Englishman, like my father, the late Frederick William Griffith, but was of ancient English stock, where our family was of Welsh descent. He was a soldier, like my grandfather Colonel Thomas Tate of the 263rd U.S.Infantry, and my eldest uncle, Captain Thomas Tate, Jr., of the 22nd New York.

His military service had been in India, in the British Army, as a Colonel of Engineers, with a period as Colonel of a regiment of Lancers. There he had married, resigned his commission, and engaged in business as owner of a tea plantation.

I believe Colonel Churchward told any
something about his marriage there. He rarely mentioned it
to me in a way to indicate how happy or unhappy it was.
The fact that he became a rover over the world for a time,
returned to England, eventually came to America and resided
here permanently, may be taken as bearing on the subject.

A traveler, who had lived in nearly every continent of earth, and seen much that was both usual and
weird and curious, he told me of many things credible and
incredible, of experiences of diverse sorts, perils, escapes, encounters. An artist, fluent, fertile, though
with manifest crudities of style reminiscent of the elementary glimmerings of perspective of the early Egyptians,
he painted and showed me in oils and water-colors, in
black and whites, scenes and peoples of many lands.

An inventor, as my father was, they had much in
common in that plane. A rough diamond physicist, he fired
my young brain with devices and mechanical movements, tricky
contrivances which afterward I found in books and factories
and copies of patents, but then were to me just the outpourings of the well-stored and ingenious mind of the Colonel.

A fisherman who made it a hobby and a science
in itself, he taught me all I ever knew about the angler's
art. We went out in small boats in the ocean for bluefish
and mackerel, but mostly in fresh water for bass and pickerel, pike, perch, and trout. At heart the Colonel scorned
the salt-water angler as a "broom-stick and clothesline

fisherman", and found little thrill outside of the delicacy and finesse of light rods and light tackle, flies for trout and bass, trolling or casting spoons for the rest. Wading in heavy hip boots in streams, rowing flat-bottomed boats in clear lakes and rivers. Taking your catch by skill of high order, from water you could drink, diluted with some old Rye or Bourbon.

At that time, before the wrinkles of age and the buffets of the Steel Juggernaut had dimmed his lustre, Colonel Churchward was a distinguished figure. Above medium height, sturdily built, with the eye of a hawk, a military bearing, an aquiline nose, a firm regular mouth set in the tensity of command, but breaking out constantly into a cheery, winning smile. The well-shaped head of the thinker, just a trifle more meso-cephalic than dolicho-cephalic, the head of the man of affairs and culture. A smooth healthy complexion, rosy cheeks, a moderately bull-dog chin clothed in a trimmed beard turning iron-gray.

His voice was at times sharp and incisive, when aroused, soft and purring when charming either man or woman. Cordially friendly and candid when conversing, persuasive when arguing or explaining. At its best when, relaxed and off guard, it was just the refined cultured English gentleman's voice speaking to his kind without intent other than to discourse and give unself-conscious expression to his own genial personality.

His years of sojourn in India, with many English soldiers, and utterly innumerable Sikhs and Ghoorkas under him, dozens of Hindu servants, each specialized in the manner of the country to his particular job, had given the Colonel, if indeed he hadn't been born with it, a power and habit of command of men and events, a will to rule, an indomitable determination added to an equally invincible persistency.

An unusual personality, many-facetted, with attainments and potentialities such as might have elevated him to the heights. Whenever and wherever in life, any measure of success with its access of power came to him, Colonel Churchward displayed his stature and possibilities of expression. But disasters and defeats, much as he courageously fought them, shrank him and cramped his growth and climbing; diminished him in will and in physique.

With a remarkable innate capacity for attracting friends and supporters, partners and associates, a nature which radiated kindness and friendship, there was coupled a thirty third degree efficiency in "the gentle art of making enemies."

Anticipating the great American prophet Farley's "Call me Jim", the Colonel was by his own will and common habitude "Churchey" to all of us; to old and new friends, business acquaintances, attorneys, all ages of men and women and children. From the first day and words I ever spoke to him, I am sure I called him "Churchey", and have no recollection of ever, either in childhood or later life, calling him anything else.

Colonel Churchward was born in England, of an old Devonshire family of gentlemen, who had lived in Devonshire since before they bore the name. In the thirteenth century this family, whose previous name is unknown, was given by Royal appointment and Ecclesiastical designation the permanent role and privilege of churchwardens to an extensive territory. The name, first Churchwarden, arose from this rank and standing in Devonshire. To Devon they clung, and to the traditions and customs of Devon. Of them might be said generally what an old Devon farmer whom Churchey introduced to me here, said to him: "Davonshire thee bist, James, and Davonshire thee'lt all's be, gin thee bist in the Staates all thee's lahfe".

Certain authorities fix the function of churchwarden in the 14th century at earliest. There is, however, ample evidence that this very important appointment was made over 700 years ago, and that the family has held the name for that period. The main members of the Churchward family, or those left by inheritance in possession, occupy the second oldest house in all England.

Colonel Churchward showed adherence to the traditions of his family, in being a rather devout Christian, supporting literally in argument every word of the old and new Testaments of the Hebrew and Christian Bibles. Though where they conflicted with his views on Mu, and the length of time he allotted to the Muan or Mayan development, he shrugged them aside or dismissed them with a specious sentence. He was a pronounced Creationist and denounced the idea of Evolution, but embraced it unconsciously wherever it helped any theory of his own.

He spoke with mingled pride and disapproval of a mildly famous member of the Churchward family, the Hedley Churchward who in the Victorian era, after exploring and traveling the Orient, particularly the Near East, abandoned Christianity publicly and became a Mohammedan. He and Colonel Churchward corresponded often. Churchey told me Hedley was vastly older than he, but I recall that the apostate only died some eight years before the Colonel.

Hedley Churchward (I forget what relation he was to James) became known to the Arabs as Mahmoud Churchward. His apostasy shocked Queen Victoria, who I am told visited some branch of the Churchward family in Devon. Churchey told me that the Queen learned to love plaice on a visit there. Plaice are flat fish, including flounders and other kindred. It was regarded at London as a very common or not genteel species of fish for Her Majesty, so she had her chef skin the plaice and cook them with trimmings to disguise what they were.

Professor Ernest Weekley, an authority on English surnames, cited the Churchward family as having retained their surname for seven centuries unchanged, which is true if we overlook that it was doubtless Churchwarden at first, before the tip end of its tail got cut off. Other members of the family were prominent in exploring and science, and in writing of it.

Colonel Churchward's elder brother Dr. Albert Churchward M.D., M.R.C.I., F.R.G.S., was a prolific writer on Freemasonry and its relation to primitive mankind, and on the origin and evolution of man. He was a well-known English physician with a large general practice, also an ethnologist, physicist, author, member of the Royal Societies, a metallurgist, arms expert and moderate philosppher. Some of his books are to be found in libraries in all parts of the world.

There were other Churchwards he told me of, who had been active in the Far East and the South Seas. One, William B. Churchward, who was some relative of his, was British Consul at Samoa while the Colonel was in India and the Pacific, and went on a long jaunt for some years through the Navigators' Islands section. I believe James either went with him or met him there, but I know that William remained for several years, and the restless James didn't.

Then there was a Spencer Churchward who made philological and other explorations among the Polynesians. Also a Robert Churchward who afterward, in 1932, led the Matto Grosso expedition in search of Lieut.Col.P.H.Fawcett in South America, whom they failed to locate. And some others he spoke of whose names escape me.

For most of their long lives Jim and Al Churchward were inseparable. They studied the same things, and though one elected the medical profession and the other engineering and the military, and were separated by oceans, they maintained regular correspondence, saw each other on Jim's trips to England and when their paths crossed in the Orient, or they explored together in far lands.

Later, they quarreled bitterly. I have never had opportunity to know Dr. Churchward's side of that, but there is good reason to believe that in this at least Colonel Churchward was right. His first attempt to make an armor plate to surpass the then standard "Harveyized" steel alloy, was based on formulae furnished him by his brother, who had done some work on them in the well-known Vickers-Maxim plant,

But this was a high-nickel-content alloy, and presented such practical and technical difficulties that, whether patentably new or not, it did not appear to the Colonel and other steel men here, to be worth while following up. Later, in the War, a high-nickel alloy was used largely in certain airplane parts.

Colonel Churchward abandoned the high-nickel alloy, and went on to a newer development. There was no connection between the two, as the state of the art then stood. But, like many inventors, the Doctor felt that his idea had started the whole thing, forgetting that there were a score of known alloys which would far better have suggested to anyone to work on the lines the Colonel followed, and the Colonel in none of his steel inventions, used anything of the original invention of his brother, if indeed there was novel and patentable matter in it.

The long association of the two brothers was of great value to the Colonel, presumably to both. It aided and directed his development along lines which led him to the measure of fame and success he attained, although in equity he deserved more of both in at least some part of his life-achievements.

Colonel Churchward was educated at Oxford and also at Sandhurst Royal Military College. His boyhood life I know only in snatches. He was quite young, vigorous, virile, vital and handsome when, as an officer in the British Army, he was sent to India. He saw active service there in conflicts with border tribes, and in minor rebellions or riots. But in the main it was Kiplingesque army routine and British social life.

The earliest pictures I have seen of him were photos and brilliantly colored miniatures painted from them by himself, in his gorgeously ornate uniforms as Colonel of his regiment. A striking figure you'd never forget. The man of later American life most people have seen, was but a shadow of that Churchward I knew as a boy. Faded, diminished, even his clear blue eyes had paled. Often, glancing at him and recalling him as he was, I have wondered whether some great physical or mental blow or shock, some social or family or financial debacle, had struck him at some time or other outside my ken. There was a long period when, in an over-busy life, I saw nothing of him, except hurried calls in apparent distress for funds.

It couldn't have been solely his ragged experiences in Steel, (which I shall recite hereinafter) which had so transformed this man of steel himself; for this radical change had in part taken place before I made him his first fortune in Steel, hence before his subsequent annihilation by the final crash engineered by certain inner forces in Steel and High Finance.

After my father died, at my tender age of five,

Colonel Churchward, who was a hound for heraldry and geneology, presented us with a meticulous record showing our family's descent from the last Welsh King Llewellyn, and tracing descent from the same Llewellyn, of both Henry the Eighth and, curiously enough, Katherine Howard, one of his ill-fated wives. He showed me often his own "tree", which for seven centuries was pure English, mostly Devonshire on both sides, but by a branch his family and ours had been connected by intermarriage some centuries back, though not in any line of further descent for either of us.

"Churchey" was an alert, lively, talkative, jolly fellow, of the breed of "life of the party". He was a welcome visitor to our home from my boyhood. After my father's death, he was one of those many loyal and interesting persons who constantly called at our home at a time when our resources and conditions afforded him nothing but friendship of a simple order without material advantages.

Young as I was, I recall looking out of the window at the monster drifts of snow, in the blizzard of March 1888, which reached above the high front stoop and the first-floor sills, and seeing the Colonel, then a man of middle age, staggering through the blockade of snow, puffing clouds of smoke from his proudly-colored meerschaum, and finally landing inside the house.

He unloaded from his stout shoulders a large ham, four loaves of bread, a stone firkin of butter, and a gallon can of milk, and said half-apologetically to all of us, "I know they're not delivering goods from the shops, so I thought I'd better stop off here and bring along these things, in case you might be running short of supplies."

My mother, daughter of the Colonel Thomas Tate previously mentioned, of the old New York colonial family identified with the City in those days when her father and grandfather Grant Thorburn knew everyone residing in town who was a native (days when the white marble City Hall was left with a brownstone back because "no one lived up that way except country-folk on their farms "), never forgot this act of Churchey's, nor did any of us. She often referred to it, and in far later years, when Churchey was down and dispirited, aided him, as both my brother and I did in many ways, both financially and by constantly reminding him that any Griffith home was always open to him to drop in and dine or just chat, at any time.

Never once did any one of us say no to any appeal of Churchey's for funds to carry him over the rough places Life gave him too frequently. We took very seriously that blizzard experience; it was no small distance from his home to ours, all conveyances were stopped, and progress through the high drifts of snow was slow and difficult. The episode is one of the many illumines the character of the man, and also reasons why we helped him with his steel and other matters; and why I have deferred even this matter of straightening out the Continent of Mu question until now, when an old friend's feelings cannot be hurt by a sifting of the truth from the residue for the permanent records of science and literature,

(I need not reiterate my feeling that my doing this is of advantage to his fame and standing.)

Churchey had taken hours to reach our house. Fiercely-fought hours, against tremendous obstacles. His cheeks were red as the muffler wound around his ears, but his smile was as boyish, sitting in front of the cannel-coal fire thawing out, as though he had just been playing a game of cricket or Rugby. All his packages were wet, as he had set them down to save some woman who had collapsed in the snow but a block from her house, whom he had carried to her door, stumbling through the drifts. Saved her life, as we learned afterward from her own story.

This was all perfectly typical of Churchey. It is also equally characteristic of him that when, in later life, he told of this exploit, he so amplified it that his burden had seemingly, if we assemble his various tales of it, been something like this:

    2 hams
    1 saddle of mutton
    1 15-lb turkey
    1 hindquarter of beef
    1 haunch of venison
    1 20-lb pickerel (caught through the ice)
    1 hundredweight of flour
    1 case of wine
    1 hamper of game pies, caviar, etc.
    1 basket of assorted vegetables
    1 barrel of apples
    1 keg of cider
    1 packing-case filled by the bake-shop
    1 barrel of potatoes
 and various other articles of food-necessity or luxury.

Not because Churchey was a liar, or purposely misstated facts, but because he was a born fisherman, and adept, an habitue, an angler-addict; and as such it was second nature for him to spin out any yarn, as any good fisherman knows every other good fisherman than himself always does.

Churchey read and recited to me English nonsense verses of Edward Lear, Lewis Carroll's Alice and Hunting the Snark, which neither my brother Ed nor myself thought quite so screamingly funny as he did. And he would sing us snatches of old folk-songs of his native Devonshire. Then indeed I would be convulsed with laughter at his comical rendition of such silly stuff as:

> I married my wife in the full o' the moon;
> Nickeldy nuckeldy, now, now, now!
> An hour too late and a day too soon,
> Oh nickeldy nuckeldy, iddicabiddity, widdicadiddity,
> now, now, now, now, now, now !
>
> Then I milked the cow i' th' auld mon's boots;
> Nickeldy nuckeldy, now, now, now !
> An' I threw 'em ower th' chimney-coots,
> Oh nickeldy nuckeldy, iddicabiddity, widdicadiddity,
> now, now, now, now, now, now !

with many, many others quite as bucolic and quaint. And a long ballad, beginning:

> I dreamt last night that the night before,
> Two tabby cats came knocking at my door.
> I went down to let them in,
> Fell downstairs and broke my shin.
>
> Off to the doctor's I must go;
> Went there fast, though I came back slow.
> Out came the doctor, armed with a lance;
> Now, you little beggar, I'll make you dance.

But Churchey was not always clowning. An ardent English Christian gentleman, he often quoted me his family motto from his crest, "Suaviter in modo, fortiter in re", which had been theirs centuries before the time that it became trite. He always urged me to aim high, never let anyone else top me in school, using the argument that, as an

English son of an Englishman, I must not permit any mere American lad to beat me.

I agreed with all this except the assumption that I was English, when I was born in New York, of an American mother, and once in a spirit of fun told him so, adding: "I could never want anyone to think me an Englishman, Churchey, as all the Englishmen who have immigrated here, notoriously came over without a whole shirt on their backs". Fire shot from the Colonel's eyes, as he bitterly denounced this as an insolent childish Yankee lie. But broke out into a lusty laugh when I retorted, "It's true. Only half the shirt is on their back, the other half is on their front."

III.

CHURCHWARD, LE PLONGEON, MU, RAZOR KING GILLETTE AND SOME OTHERS

INVENTIONS WERE CERTAINLY NOT ALIEN to my childhood. My father had invented printing-presses and paper-feeding machinery for cylinder presses, for which the valuable American and British patents were, upon his death, found diverted from his ownership, despite the probability that he had not intentionally disposed of them. Also, among other devices, the sponson canoe and lifeboat, which he was dissuaded from patenting as "probably not commercially profitable". We children played with the model of this boat for years as a toy.

Churchey very rightly advised that it be patented, by my mother as Executrix, but she was averse to putting in the required money when my father had not. Churchey had many inventions of his own which he talked over with all of us, but his chief ones, which he patented, came later.

Our home had always been a Sunday afternoon meeting-place for people of thirst for learning, devotees of the fine arts, poets, musicians, thinkers. My father, who read with equal facility French, German, Italian, Latin and Greek, was a student of literature, versed in ancient history and antiquities, with an unusual library and a mind even better-stocked. Unlike Churchey, who sought new theories and deductions, lighting and nursing new ideas as he would smoke a cigar, my father dwelt on authors and what each had said and contributed, loving literature and belles lettres for themselves alone, with no yearning to dispossess authorities of the ages by replacing their conclusions with others, though this didn't prevent his enjoying conflicts with them if he could set equal or better authorities against them.

Even my infant memory is stamped with the impression of those crowded parlors Sundays, the clouds of fragrant blue smoke, with my father's coal-black dry crackling Havana and his fluent Oxford-accented sentences, equally conspicuous, amid the steady flow and interchange of ideas by the convection currents of converse.

While his death and our changes of residence broke up these extensive congregations, many old friends continued to come as before. In our home Churchey met scientists, engineers, journalists, composers, poets, men and women of affairs.

Churchey was himself possessed of a good voice

and a magnificent and costly orchestra flute. With the
accompaniment of some other good musician on the piano, or
of my mother or elder sister, he could with this instrument play by ear or note any opera or classical piece,
standard ballad, anything he had heard or could read and
try out a bit. American popular songs he ridiculed, yet
I have listened to him countless times accompany the famous old composer Monroe H. Rosenfeld, immortal for his
Climbing Up the Golden Stairs, Oh Dem Golden Slippers,
The Whistling Coon (which every grocer's lad in New York
whistled more incessantly than any later Yes We Have No
Bananas), and hosts of sentimental ballads and songs.

Rosenfeld, of whom Ted Marks tells clever anecdotes in his volume of musical reminiscences, played
on all of us a very excellent joke. He brought with him
different girls at times, to whom he was most transiently
devoted, each one being officially his fiancee. One night
he brought a young miss of eighteen named Kathleen, timid,
fragile, but hopelessly enthralled by the dashing Monroe,
though I recall him as far from handsome. Touched by the
devotion in the child's eyes, my mother found opportunity
to speak to him: "Oh, Rosey, she's so young and sweet and
innocent. Don't make her lose it all. Send her back to
her home, Rosey. You don't need to let this child wreck
her life."

Churchey, who had already hinted as much to
Monroe, presented the composer with a dainty miniature

in oils which he had painted on a porcelain disk, which Rosenfeld had admired almost to distraction and which Churchey had just brought that evening to show the various friends present. "Here, Monroe, I'll give you this as ransom for the little Kathleen. You've got all the girls you need, but you haven't got anything like my Frail Dryad."

Monroe protested that his interest in the beautiful Kathleen was strictly platonic, he wouldn't have brought her to our home if it were not so, she was just a girl friend, daughter of friends of his in Indiana. But he accepted the miniature, and the next time he came to us, sat down and played the lovely and still famous "I'll Take You Home Again, Kathleen", and whispered to my mother, "I took her back home again. And then I wrote this. Do you like it?"

We listened intently to what we all felt was a living, lasting composition. Churchey offered to stake him in having it published, but Monroe evaded this offer, saying he could get all the publishers he wanted for it. He frequently wrote songs under other names, for various reasons of policy, and I never suspected (questioned?) the truth of his claim to Kathleen for many years. Not until the expert and kindly Ted Marks opened my eyes by showing me that Kathleen's composer was a real man, not an alias for Monroe, and that the piece had been copyrighted two or three decades before Monroe had fooled us.

This was not an unusual prank of Monroe Rosenfeld, who was a rare joker, a fellow of bubbling good humor, quips and Rabelaisian epigrams. I may dare another digression to place this minor biographical material of record about a pioneer of modern American music. When I was fifteen and sixteen, I wrote some fiction as bad from present standards as much magazine fiction was then. Rosenfeld acted as my literary agent on a unique basis. He always paid me in cash for my stories, which he managed to get published in obscure sheets. Never any cheques to my order. He was quite frank about it. " The real work is getting it sold, Perc. I take out what I think my share, and give you what the rubbish was worth. Any time you feel you're not getting enough, tell me." My early entry into business prevented my long continuing this partnership.

Churchey could discuss any question on earth with any expert or exponent of it. He might be wrong or right, but he was intelligent and keen. Jolly, laughing, with a fund of humorous stories smacking of the old English countryside and taverns, and much folk-lore, British and foreign. Besides which, he was stocked with a jumble of broad-scoped fundamental knowledge and fantastic and wild notions all too much commingled. To many men with conventional yardsticks and acid tests he didn't always measure up.

Among those to whom I introduced him at our house were two whose acquaintance led him to his later devotion to the Continent of Mu, to the series of volumes about its people. These were the old Professor Augustus Le Plongeon, (born in 1826) and his younger and devoted wife and ex-ploring-companion Madame Alice Le Plongeon. The Le Plongeons were explorers and archaeologists who had made discoveries startling and sensational in Yucatan, and uncovered parts of the now famous and well-worked buried ruins of Chichen Itza.

Time had passed. I had grown to tall adolescence, and made an early dive into business. Finishing grammar school at the age of twelve, I entered High School, but feeling that the family finances were then most discouraging and would become steadily leaner, I left high school and secured a job as office boy in a law office devoted to patents and inventions. Here for four years I studied patent law, Patent Office practice, inventions, machinery, mechanical movements, physics, chemistry, electricity and a melange of technical matters in my spare hours. I was greatly helped by books Churchey lent me, and by chats with him. His views, as I afterward reviewed them, were most unorthodox, but they aroused my interest.

Churchey often came in to sit and smoke and talk with me, in an office where he met many inventors. Among them Oscar Hammerstein, who was patenting cigar-making machinery, which he sold out to good advantage, and made his first rise from the cigar-maker's bench to the rank of a financier, an investor in cigar and tobacco corporations and plantations, a partner in the famed Vaudeville or

Variaties firm of Koster & Bial, then the builder of Hammerstein's Victoria Theatre, an impresario and rebel in New York Opera in competition with the Metropolitan.

Hammerstein had a decidedly strong influence upon the office boy for his patent lawyers in a way he didn't quite anticipate. Besides my studies on technical subjects, I read many French novels, partly for the language practice. Seeing me with Zola's L'Assommoir, Hammerstein reproved me mildly, advising me "if you read that stuff now, you'll leave yourself no new sensations when you grow up. Stick to normal American and English fiction." He presented me with volumes of Goethe and Schiller, and Von Humboldt's Cosmos, which were far from being the fiction he recommended. They led me to repair to the Public Library, where I made out a list of the heaviest scientific and philosophical reading matter a youngster ever punished himself with, and from the very beginning of my self-imposed course, I was both a lost child and one who had found his road and his Mecca, his Lady Fair and his Holy Grail. All of which he must, despite the calls of business and money, of sport, the dance or romance, the empty bladder of society, so-called, pursue unceasingly.

Thus when our friends the Le Plongeons returned one year from their protracted stay in Yucatan, with glowing accounts of their newer discoveries there, with fragments of ancient architectural works there, photos of marvelous and curious relics of a civilization allegedly more than double the Biblical age of the world, I listened with an ear attuned to their music. I drank it all in and felt neither hunger nor thirst, except for more of their story, nor marked the passage of Time in contemplation of the aeons spread before me in their eloquent narratives.

Churchey, the two Le Plongeons and I spent many hours together discussing Yucatan, the Mayans, and the origins of civilization. We four, or five when my mother was joined with us, were mostly alone in our intrigued obsession with the fascinating subject. No other member of my family circle ever seemed to care a rap for science, and guests who listened with interest, passed easily to other matters of more immediate appeal to them.

If it had not been for Churchey's eager willingness to talk Yucatan and the Mayans with the Le Plongeons, there would have been little chance for me to hear so much from them, as a mere boy. They gave out streams of facts about their life-study, and were posted on it as never any other people I ever met. Yet even then I knew there was some atmosphere of scepticism in the scientific world about the Le Plongeons.

They were indubitably the first to penetrate the Yucatan wilderness and the secrets of the ancient Mayan civilization, and make revelation of the amazing facts discovered. Their lectures and publications, communications to learned societies, had astonished archaeologists and scientists generally, and led to later expeditions which have made sophomore knowledge of what was then terra incognita.

The old professor, with his long white flowing beard, was a solemn figure, and the earnest winning speech and personality of Madame Alice Le Plongeon was a charming and contrasting complement. My lack of years made it impossible for me rightly to appraise the scientific distrust which finally estopped the Le Plongeons from complete recognition and support of future work by them. An eminent archaeologist, after sponsoring the Professor, told me "the man is a pseudo-scientist ". In return, Le Plongeon taught me fifty Mayan words, which I was to try out on the critic, and reveal that this great man did not in fact know as much Mayan as a boy of fifteen had acquired. I never summoned up nerve enough to essay this.

I have heard many men called pseudo-scientists. Men termed Colonel Churchward that to me, and Steel men declined to admit that he was a Steel expert or a reliable metallurgist in the same day that they sold his great steel surreptitiously and pocketed the money. Herbert Spencer, with whom I corresponded as a young man, was vastly delighted when some opponent now lost in deserved oblivion, called him "an empty sciolist". Graham Bell was threatened with arrest in Philadelphia for trying to induce men to invest in such an obvious swindle as his telephone. Edison once told me that the opposition of men in authority in science and technology, who ridiculed his pretensions to knowledge of physics and electrical science, had "erected barriers in my path almost at times unsurmountable ". Alan Hawley said to me that when the Wrights were endeavoring to get the French Government to build just one of the planes which a dozen years later were flying in thousands over French armies, Hawley took Wilbur Wright up in a balloon over Paris, and listened to him outline what he believed the heavier than air device would become in the world. And he confided to me that " I felt I was up in that balloon with a man absolutely looney, and had a strong desire to pull the rip-cord and get down to earth quickly. I left that balloon with a sigh of relief."

Le Plongeon and Churchward being both Masons well-versed in its mysteries and lore, spent much time in conversations upon this to me unknown subject. Masonry made Churchey not only many friends, but served him valuably in his adventures in Steel, which I shall describe hereafter. The two scientists, or Pseudo-scientists, had much in common, therefore, besides Yucatan, and the Mayans.

Le Plongeon had found in Yucatan evidences of the immigration of the Mayans into Yucatan from a mother-country called Mu, which he identified with Plato's lost Atlantis. (Mu having been located in the Pacific and later in the Atlantic Ocean regions) This was claimed to have been the centre of world-civilization, and engulfed by a flood due to earthquake and subsidence.

If all Le Plongeon's narratives and discoveries presented were genuine and authentic, his work was of vast importance to the world. When I spoke to Churchey about the attacks on Le Plongeon, he was quite on the fence. One day Le Plongeon was a venerated and great explorer, and his critics all jealous. Another time, he shrugged his shoulders, said Le Plongeon didn't know half as much as he pretended, and had acquired much on the Mayans and Mu from past records about them. This Le Plongeon (openly himself) declared.

In discussing Le Plongeon with many, I aroused the curiosity of King C. Gillette, then an inventor of kegs and such things, small improvements in beer-containers or bottling devices. As a boy, I had warmed to King Gillette from my first meeting with him. He was a client for years of the firm of patent attorneys I worked for, but not in any steady business. When he drifted into the office and waited for one of the firm to come in, or be at liberty, he cocked up his long legs on a desk and chatted with me as though I were an adult. King was a mild Socialist at that time. He looked on the existing arrangement of Capitalism as repugnant, but would not disrupt it entirely. No anarchism and bloody revolutions, no barricades and death to the bourgeois. His remedy was to organize the whole world into a vast corporation, in which every man would own just one share of stock. He could orate fluently on social injustice for hours.

Much taken by my talk of the Le Plongeons, King accepted an invitation to my home to meet them, and frequently dropped in. He had already met Churchey in my office. King came of excellent family, one brother George being an inventor like himself, another comptroller of an insurance company. King brought his very amiable and lovable mother one night. She was, among other activities, authoress of the then famous White House Cook Book, still sold by the thousands, of which she gave my mother a copy.

Gillette however, turned thumbs down on both my friend Churchey and Le Plongeon. He believed the Le Plongeons had magnified their own discoveries. As Churchey disputed this with him, he felt the old soldier was also one that "laid it on too thick". Once when Churchey was holding the floor rather long with descriptions of his life in India and certain mysteries of the Buddhist priests, King turned to me and said a trifle unpleasantly, "Perc, isn't it about time Churchey allowed the rest of us to sit in and draw cards?"

King Gillette struck fortune as one strikes oil or gold suddenly. By opportunity coupled with swift grasp of it. He was retained as expert witness in one of our patent cases involving a bottle-stopper. One day he went over to the opposite side and took employment with them. Became interested in their new Crown seal for bottles, since and now used in the hundreds of millions. He took the New England Agency for it, and made an immense income.

The way he hit on the celebrated razor which earned him the sobriquet of Razor King Gillette, and placed his picture and autograph "in more cities, towns, villages or hamlets than those of any other living or dead man", was equally fortuitous. His brother George was experimenting upon a sheep-shearing machine which eventually, I believe became successful. The first trial, as I recall, necessita-

corrections — JTG

ted mercifully shooting the sheep. "That's not the right principle", said King. He started to invent one himself. He quit in disgust, but meanwhile applied his ideas of shearing devices to a safety razor instead, and presto! the great Gillette razor was born.

In later years, King Gillette loomed across our horizon in two ways, one in connection with an attempt by Colonel Churchward to enlist him in Steel, and the other through Egbert Gold of Chicago Car Heating fame, who did himself back the Colonel and was my staunch supporter in that enterprise. Of which anon.

In outlining the matters both direct and collateral, which had powerful bearing upon Colonel Churchward's life and work, and which must be understood to analyse and appraise his work on Mu, his contribution to industry in his great N C V Steel, and to supply such record of his biography as I can offer, I am adhering to proper sequence and chronology.

By so doing, this intimate exposition and eclaircissement of both his Steel adventure and the final turning to the Continent of Mu, will be briefer, clearer and most easily followed.

There is a temptation to go more deeply into the Mu matter at this very point of our joint discussions of it with the Le Plongeons, but just as Mu was the climax of his life-work, it is more appropriate and orderly to dispose of the matters and steps in the Colonel's career which alone ~~make~~ render it possible to appraise and make comprehensible his arriving at the writing of The Lost Continent of Mu, to effectually complete an exact assay of the metal in his work, beyond further dispute, or other interpretation.

IV.

CHURCHEY, SPIKES AND TIE-PLATES, PATENTS AND ME.

AFTER RESIGNING HIS commission in India, and leaving the Army for the vocation of a tea planter, Colonel Churchward momentarily prospered. While mostly he was silent upon his own family life in those years, and in his early years in America, of the Army life there, battles, escapes, the Hindus, houses and servants, fishing, hunting, he freely spoke a thousand items.

In his tea experience, owing to some bad season or other cause, monetary difficulties overtook him. He greatly blamed certain British-Indian bankers for his downfall. He claimed to have trusted them and they had squeezed or "rooked" him.

This disheartening episode undoubtedly colored his views of business relations saffron. In America, I know of no business he was ever in, that someone or some group hadn't allegedly "gypped" or "rooked" him. Was it true? In Steel, to my knowledge, and yours when you finish my brief description of it, Colonel Churchward did not receive a square deal. To what extent this was the result of individual acts of anyone, or any company, and to what it was due to the system and conditions which constitute Steel, the Industry, High Finance, and our Courts, one need not attempt to particularize, and I at no place herein shall do so. But was this the case with all and sundry of Churchey's affairs? There were conflicting stories.

Upon coming to America, he engaged in railroad work as a civil engineer, and soon was connected with an active concern selling railway supplies of all kinds, from lock-nuts, spikes and tie-plates up to the biggest articles of equipment in the limits of maintenance of way. He traveled the whole country selling these goods and was moderately successful in his profits and actual sales. But he boasted of his contracts like a fisherman describing his catch. I am sure Diamond Jim Brady, who traded in his wake decades afterward, with millions of dollars of sales annually, never approached the reported big deals the Colonel loved to tell us about. It was this factor more than any other, that alienated King Gillette from Churchey; like many more, he hated to be made to listen to it.

Churchward met Railroad Presidents and Superintendents, assistant superintendents of maintenance and right of way men, engineers, conductors, brakemen, and fascinated one and all of them. Churchey to them all, he took them and their families fishing, showed them how, and made quick friendships everywhere. He would send fish packed in ice from Maine to presidents with whom he had previously fished in Michigan, and minor presents to their wives.

He fell out, however, with the heads of the firm with whom he was associated. His denunciation was bitter, as usual, but others told me the firm members were just as bitter, and specific in their criticisms. Churchey went through a long period of ill-luck and hard times. He did not wholly lose his spirits and his optimism. Having railroad passes, he continued to go on short fishing trips, and I often went with him. He would come to our home Sundays and odd evenings, and to smoke and chat in my place of employment.

Churchward now invented some useful and efficient railway spikes and tie-plates. Spikes to nail down the rails into the wooden ties, plates to set under the rails, with spike-holes in them, to hold the rails, save the ties, prolong them, make for better safety. Churchward's devices prevented the rails cutting off the spike-heads, or creeping or spreading. Like most such inventions, they weren't radical departures, but they were better. He had no funds to obtain patents, but friends went in with him. He used attorneys selected by the partners, my own employers were too costly for such work, but when he had difficulties in getting his applications allowed by the Patent Office, as usually happens, I rewrote his specifications and prepared arguments which got him the patents. Boyish enthusiasm and blind faith in my hero, worked wonders.

He now was able to form a corporation of his own, with funds from friends who took stock, and despite a little rough sledding, made progress. He addressed meetings of railway men and boards of directors, and sold his goods well. His addresses and articles published in trade papers he always brought to me beforehand, and we rewrote them together. Chiefly I substituted facts for blah, and restrained and convincing arguments in lieu of scornful attacks and ridicule of competitors and their products.

Churchey one day suggested I get a better job. He introduced me flatteringly to an eminent attorney who had just lost his assistant, and gravely assured him that I, just over sixteen, could fill the position. After much hemming and hawing for weeks, the lawyer decided I was too young for any client to listen to or deal with.

I became indignant at this, and at once borrowed some small funds from a relative and opened up an office for myself to take out patents. Churchey stoutly supported my boldness, and without his enthusiasm I should never have had the nerve to do it. It was a mad venture for a boy, and its success was more than I had the right to expect. Churchey promised to get me business from many sources (none came from his efforts till after I was established), and to take out all his own patents through me (I never took a fee from him, though I accepted one from his son who insisted on paying for a patent I secured for him, for a marine torpedo.)

Sixteen, I was too young to be admitted to the bar, but there was then no restriction as to patent attorneys practicing before the U.S. Patent Office to take out patents, nor in the foreign patent offices. When I became twenty one, I was instrumental in obtaining the establishment of a Patent Office registration system, since when no man can practice there unless qualified. I am still registered as an attorney there, though not engaged now in active practice.

Oddly, it prospered. Thousands of inventors came to me, and took out patents. Soon the business was so good, the capital-providing relative came in with me, taking (as elders will do and youngsters permit) too heavy a share of the gate receipts. My entry into patent practice revolutionized it in at least one way. Old fogies had taken too long to get an inventor his patent. Everything dragged. Proceedings were protracted and wearisomely discouraging. I inaugurated the plan of prompt action, getting each case drawn and filed at once, and answering Patent Office objections quickly. For a long while, it became possible for one to get a patent when the idea was hot and the time ripe to market it. Today things have drifted back into longer delays. It is astonishing to recall that I secured patents allowed in some cases in nine or sixteen days after filing them. Churchey had advised me that this was what inventors wanted and didn't get, and to work hard for strong patents speedily obtained.

I was now able in many ways to help my old friend. He was quite hard up and I loaned him money from time to time, to keep above water. I never once refused a touch from him, and never asked a cent back or kept track of it all.

He was still, as always, too boastful and talkative about his supposed deals and sales and prospects. In my home and offices he would brag to anyone of "sweeping the field" with his spike and tie-plate, and of the immense contracts landed. I had to caution him that friends and strangers alike distrusted these tall stories. Perhaps a third his age, I still ventured to point out that he talked too injudiciously, and would not get into quarrels with his associates if he made it a fetish to satisfy them and treat them fairly.

I showed him the six rules I had at sixteen pasted in my desk-drawer to govern my business life, which I do not apologize for making place for here, as they may be of more value to some one person than all the rest of my account:

    1. Never make a man a proposition to which in his shoes you would not yourself say yes.
    2. Never write or say anything you would not willingly see in big print in the papers, and stand by.
    3. Give every man, besides all you agreed to, some one thing which neither of you had mentioned.
    4. Handle each man's matters as though he were your most important customer, and lifelong best friend.
    5. For fear of overstating anything, understate everything.
    6. Never put yourself in a cul de sac.

Churchey dismissed all these maxims as being exactly what he habitually did himself ! Except the fifth, which he ridiculed roundly. "Bosh and twaddle, Perc ! When I landed here, I found you Americans bragged and enlarged everything, and I had to, also, to keep my end up. Everyone adds a few inches to his fish, or nobody here thinks it was big enough to talk about."

Facts like this must be known and borne in mind in appraising and analysing the Churchward of his later life-events.

We continued our fishing trips. By this time, these expeditions were arranged on the basis that Churchey provided the railway passes which his business gave him, and I paid the hotel bills, boatmen and other costs. Tackle of all kinds he could always have for the asking, from firms to whom he directed innumerable customers met on his jaunts.

In many of these trips, as extensively in his life outside of his hours with me or my family, Churchey was a dashing and winning man with women. By your own fireside, or in that of his big customers, he was circumspect and most perfectly well-behaved and correct, showing his breeding and traditions. But in his rambles through fields and forest and the shores of rivers and lakes, he was an exponent of the proverb "Les aventures arrivent aux aventuriers ".

As a fisherman, if there were fish in the waters, Churchey got them. This statement fits his bonnes fortunes also. He would mislead no young girl, nor make passes at the wives and daughters of his friends. Neither did he demean himself with women of the streets or brothels. If one asks, "who and what then were left?" the answer is "plenty". His success was remarkable. He was no ascetic, and he found a cordial reception to his affections widely bestowed.

In a romantic spot in Ohio, where the trout leaped, and the heart of youth leaped with them and with wild nature threaded by running waters, Churchey introduced me to my first actual sweetheart, in the person of a young, dainty but not previously wholly ingenue rosy-cheeked girl, sixteen like myself, adorable and forever memorable, despite that for over a quarter century she lies with the Alice of Ben Bolt in perennial girlish loveliness in all the hearts that beat with hers, perpetuated by the one sure means we possess of preserving the image of youth from the decay of age.

Churchey had a fund of experiences and stories of them in this connection, in and from many countries. I learned much of the distinguishing features and sex-habits of Hindu girls from him. He often spun yarns which were obviously fictional or expanded, but invariably I could discern the difference. When he was narrating a factual incident in his own life, his manner and tones became completely altered. When he drew a long bow, it was as if he were a minor actor impersonating a raconteur or swashbuckler; but hewing close to the line of truth, he was a simple narrator of unvarnished facts by an unprejudiced witness.

Once he showed me the nude photo of a prominent European princess, taken when she was young, and told me of his first meeting with her at a lawn party in England. They strolled off to a woodsey patch, chatting. Suddenly, as they paused in the shadows, he seized her boldly in a manner best here described as dangerously venturesome and likely in most cases to provoke screams for help. She gazed at him from beneath her dark lashes, and exclaimed in her prettily accented English, "You flirt, you!" I was so sure Churchey was telling me the exact truth, that I was little if at all surprised when one night he showed me a letter from her which referred to the episode unmistakably.

Characteristically, Churchey fell out with his new backers in the corporation and was brimful of squeals of having been "rooked". But as these men were equally vociferous against him, I don't know who was at fault. Churchey could never see any side other than his own, nor view others' acts dispassionately where they antagonized him, hence one got from him nothing but complaints ~~from him~~ in such quarrels, and no confessions.

The attorney for the opposition, an old fogy, came to me asking my aid to get Churchey to arbitrate with them. I used my offices and Churchey agreed to compromise, but failed to do so, blaming their obstinacy and greed.

Then followed one of his leanest periods. His trade and good-will in the railway field seemed to drop off, friends in and out of business drifted away, the last remnants of the aura of recent success vanished. I had no connections or influences able to aid him in any way except by just giving him money, but he continued to come to my home, flash his cheery smile, his Micawber hopes; his flute was as tuneful, his stories as thrilling.

Churchey was a chess-player far out of my novice class. He was also a skillful bridge player (at first then, it was whist) but here he wasn't supreme. At least twice weekly there would be a foursome of Churchey and my brother Ed against an uncle of ours and myself. Our team played a strictly scientific game according to the rules as the game was then, exhausting trumps, establishing the long suit, unblocking lesser cards, with conventional leads, play and signals. On the contrary, Churchey's team relied on a sort of piratical system, psychic, hope-filled, lucky breaks, establishing cross-ruffs with uncanny facility, making wild and reckless leads and finesses, and getting away with them. In the long run, of course, the psychic plays went sour, and when debacle came, Churchey would loudly throw up the sponge, play off the hand heedlessly, carelessly.

Elwell, one of the chief bridge experts of the day, playing with Churchey against us, said to me afterward, "If Colonel Churchward handled his soldiers as he plays bridge, then when he was besieged by a superior force, instead of digging in, fortifying his position, fighting cagily and retreating in order, he would blow up the city, shhot all his men and the civilians and himself as well."

My practice in patents continued to grow. Inventors sent me inventors. Prominent attorneys sent me their clients who had inventions to patent. Thomas A. Edison sent me some, including Prince Troubetskoy, the able European engineer. Judge W.M.K. Olcott turned over all his patent and trade mark clientele, feeling it was a specialty he didn't desire to handle. Foreign attorneys sent me cases to patent in America, and I sent them thousands of applications for foreign patents in return.

Churchey sent me many, after a while, including the most voluminous case I ever wrote up; the earliest invention in sending pictures and other facsimiles over wires. Its sheets of drawings covered the floor of a large room, the specifications I sent in contained forty thousand words.

At this period, Churchey participated in two of the most thrilling episodes of my whole life, one showing his courage, the other his acumen, and both his loyalty.

The first was a visit from the forever unknown inventor of the great "Hippocyclorum". I was seated in an isolated private office where I repaired to study out intricate cases, uninterrupted. The door opened and in walked, unannounced, a man who was a symphony in black. Black suit and tie, black hat, black shoes, black overcoat on his arm, black gloves in his fingers. Black hair and beard, bushy black eyebrows and lashes, black eyes like polished coals. He carried a black leather roll of drawings and a black bag.

This personage, a foreigner of some forty odd, drew a big black revolver from his pocket and laid it on the table, saying amiably, "Not at all to intimidate you, sir, but in case we were to be interrupted by some intruder.

The bag will also help in that emergency; it contains dynamite." Then as an afterthought he added, extending his hand, "Mr. Griffith, I presume. I have wanted so much to meet you and show you my invention."

I realized at once that he was of unsound mind. I smiled, shook hands, and said, "I am at the moment engaged on some cases; if you will step into our main offices and wait, I will join you shortly. " He declined, angrily. "My invention is more important than all the stuff cranks send you to patent."

He opened up his leather roll, and displayed on a long table the most beautifully executed and elaborate set of working drawings imaginable. They must have required months of work; they showed a high order of skill.

Here were countless wheels and levers, pistons, pulleys and belts, air-compressors, electric motors and circuits, solenoids, rheostats, fly-wheels and governors, one medley of all the mechanical movements and contrivances of the century. Every meshing cog-wheel was toothed accurately, and as the man explained the machine, he described the number of teeth and revolutions with precision. He traced his circuits, he described the motion of the parts.

"What is it?" I asked. "Perpetual motion?"

"Indeed no. I am aware that is impossible. This is a machine to draw power from the cosmos. I call it the Hippocyclorum. Hippo for the great horse-power it develops, cyclorum for the wheels that mostly compose it."

I had already grasped that his machinery was assembled to no actual operative purpose. The trains of gears led nowhere, the pulleys and belts had no connection with the reciprocating levers and pistons, the circuits terminated in switches that were without any effect on the operation or cessation of the machine.

I cut short his description. "All right, now if you will write that all out and bring it back with the drawings, we can go over it again for patenting." Not at all; he demurred strongly. I had seen his valuable device, and he wouldn't leave till I paid him for it.

The mere bagatelle of $7,000,000. I don't recall whether this was for the whole thing or a half interest. It was idle to protest I hadn't such a sum; he was angry, suspicious and became threatening. If I didn't buy, it must be because I wished to steal his brain-child.

Things became desperate. Finally I struck the right note. "We millionaires don't keep our money in our offices. It's in our vaults down in Wall Street." Good! That sounded reasonable. I would go get it. No, he would come too. As we left, he locked my office door and generously handed me the key. The bag he left till his return.

We walked down the single flight to the street. As we came out, I saw an officer on the corner, a hundred feet distant. My offices were on Broadway, between Murray Street and Park Place. I tried to attract the policeman, but he swung his club unseeing. My inventor, however, detected my action, and in a panic fled around the corner of Park Place. When I followed, he had vanished.

But I ran full tilt into Churchey, who was coming to my office. He cried, "Yoicks! Tally ho! Whither away and so forth?" I fell against his shoulder, somewhat shaken; I was barely nineteen. I spilled my story; we went upstairs. Churchey, who was of fine courage, was all for opening the black bag himself. When I refused, he insisted on remaining while I opened it.

There was nothing at all in it except a block of slag from an iron foundry, a package of cigarettes, and a pair of detachable cuffs. Inquiries never revealed who our inventive genius was. Was he a demented mechanical student? Or some famous engineer or inventor, whose previous inventions were valuable and widely used? Did he recover and perhaps become the inventor of machinery now known all over the earth? Or was he obscure, just a poor crazy piece of world-flotsam?

We never knew. But Churchey showed his mettle and his pure-gold friendship in that exciting event, as he did likewise in another incident into which his intercourse with me drew him, to his great delight. One illuminative of the man, and worthy of recording for itself.

V.

THE COLONEL HELPS ME SMASH A GANG OF RACKETEERS

DURING THIS TRYING TIME for my friend Churchey I encouraged him to drop in my office, as all our family did as to the home, and was thus enabled to invite him to luncheon, and keep him in touch with me. When I was too busy, I would tip some assistant to chat with him and ask him to lunch. How proud the Colonel would be to be listened to so deferentially, by some one who was a fresh audience, unused to the Colonel's eloquence and tall stories, and so most intrigued by them.

There is no basis for praise here. Had I been older or more experienced I might easily, with the income I was making, have hunted up some business I could have bought out for a few thousands, and placed Churchey in to run it. The idea never occurred to me. Possibly, if it had, I'd have been sceptical of his sticking long enough to make good, and not break it all up in conflict with associates and customers.

I did introduce him to a number of substantial clients of mine, and had him on occasions take them to lunch and get acquainted. He made friends but no connections. Among others was the very unique and likeable genius Bernarr MacFadden, then a physical instructor and publisher of the magazine Physical Culture. He made certain inventions in gymnasium and exercise devices, which I patented for him. An enthusiast for egging the nation into getting and keeping fit, Bernarr MacFadden was strongly in my good graces. I have nothing to say about his newspaper experience or his critics in that field. I do not claim to adhere to all his views.

But it would be difficult to name any other one force or person that did a fraction as much to awaken American men and women, and the youth of both sexes, from the ancient neglect of the human body and health. Space precludes comparing conditions before and after MacFadden began his work. His influence upon my health and strength were boundless. In our talks together, I grew convinced of his thesis.

Churchey did not follow me here. He cared for no exercise except wading through trout streams, or wild game-filled woods, or dashing from spot to spot in business sorties. He snorted at purposed exercise and all MacFadden's ideas. He wanted coffee and tea whenever he felt like them, at every meal and at five oclock, and smoked all day and part of the night. He quoted his brother Albert's friend the great Joe Chamberlain, that "the modern man gets all the exercise he needs walking up and down stairs." Joe, however, at 70 was a paralytic for the last years of his life, while MacFadden at 70 flies an airplane to Miami, walks twenty miles or more, has the vitality of a man of forty to fifty.

About this time there was entrenched in New York, in my twentieth year, a certain group of men claiming to be journalists, operating as a minor news agency. The chief function of this socalled agency seemed to be to collect news and sell it, not to any papers it claimed to syndicate, but to the subject of the news item, who might desire it suppressed. A surprising number of business men submitted to this racket, fearing damage to their reputations and business.

One day this outfit contacted with me. They were clever. They had been furnished with a news story about my firm, which appeared so absurd they wished to check it up. It was to the effect that we did not know how to take out patents, but lost most of our cases.

My partner and I laughed at this, showed them hundreds of patents we had secured, hundreds of letters from inventors all over the land, manufacturers, lawyers, testifying to our services.

Our visitors professed themselves satisfied, marked the article "killed" and departed smiling. Three days later, they dashed in, excited and anxious. It seemed that the head of the Agency had sailed for Bermuda, and in some way they couldn't comprehend, had revived the slanderous article, and ordered it " sent out to the 2000 papers on our lists."

The "journalists" were most apologetic. They wished me to write a reply, which they would gladly send out next day to all their papers at their own cost. But they didn't dare suppress the article, as they would lose their jobs when the head director returned from Bermuda. Unless indeed, I would buy up the story for what they could get out of it otherwise.

Inquiry developed that the price would be $500 each. I declined to bite. They threatened untold damage to my business. I told them to come back next day.

My partner and Churchey and I then conferred on the matter. My partner was all for "feeding them a couple of hundred to kill their silly article and substitute a fine write-up which they would send out to these thousands of papers, about valuable patents we had taken out for various inventors." Churchey, however, said they were rogues and he didn't believe they had any list of papers at all.

I went with my attorney Frederic Seymour, brother of Patent Commissioner John Seymour, to see my good friend Judge W.M.K.Olcott who was then the District Attorney of New York. He brought in his chief assistant John F.McIntire, afterwards Supreme Court Judge, who informed us that he had complaints about this agency but was unable to get evidence against them, as business men wouldn't risk the publicity and their reputations.

Judge Olcott appealed to me to help him.

I agreed to. Detective Chief McCluskey, then the feared nemesis of law-breakers, and Colonel Newcome of the private agency well-known at the time, prepared a trap for the men by giving them a small payment on account, marked, which detectives would catch them spending.

It involved some long trailing and twists and turns. It didn't click; they got no evidence. Olcott phoned me again to urge a new conference and plan. "We must get those fellows; there must be some way."

Churchey and I put our heads together, and jointly worked out a plan. The Colonel had in India, in contact with wily Hindu soldiers and servants, had much experience, as he often narrated, in ferreting out minor or major mysteries. Our plan was so simple all the professional detectives shrugged pityingly; it couldn't work. But it did.

In my offices was one room used to store the thousands of models of inventions of our clients. Devices and apparatus of every size and shape. Shelves of them, piles of them, cases of them. Some too heavy for one man to handle.

Churchey and I peeled off our coats, and behind locked doors, so no one spying might suspect and talk, we rigged this room up with a desk and chairs, re-arranged all the models and cases, and located hiding places for two of the cleverest of New York's plainclothes men who should be concealed back of the models

with tablets and pencils to make notes. At first we had
arranged places also for Churchey and a stenographer (not
together !) behind other machinery, but on a rehearsal
Churchey coughed twice and the stenographer sneezed, so
I stuck to the "dicks", cautioning them on that score.

        I then sent for the racketeers, and discussed fully
with them the nature of their acts. I denounced it as a
barefaced blackmail scheme. The racketeers coolly told
me to take it or leave it. They demanded payment under
threats by one of them of publicity, damage and even further attacks. Another claimed enough political influence
to get them off if any victim squealed. He mentioned a
man in the District Attorney's office. I could have
laughed in his face; the man he named had been in conference with Judge Olcott, McIntyre and myself, strongly
urging action, knew just what I was doing to trap the
men, and if he had been at all willing to help them he
could easily have tipped them off. That he hadn't done
so was a very neat and clean disproof of their claim.

        I handed the men $500 in marked bills, of which
we had made record also of the serial numbers, and as they
pocketed it, I drew an old English army revolver which
Churchey had loaned me, and gave the signal for the detectives to come out of their hiding-places. They cap-
tured the surprised racketeers and took them to a mag-
istrates' court, where they were given a hearing, held
for the Grand Jury and duly indicted.

Churchey was jubilant, and only regretted that he hadn't been concealed in that model room so he could be a witness against the men, but as his part had not been evidential, he was limited to giving me his aid and stout support throughout.

I received many letters indicating that this gang had had quite a few other victims, and also p phone calls from persons who would not give their own names, who said they had paid money to the men, for immunity from attack. Judge McIntyre sent me a glowing letter in his own hand, The Grand Jury thanked me, the Foreman saying he had heard of the parties before and been hoping someone would trap them.

A few friends of one of the guilty men threatened me if I would not withdraw the complaint. They departed when I gave orders to "lock the door and phone for the police". One of them went to Churchey, and offered him money to induce me to let them off. The doughty Colonel promptly knocked him down, in high rage.

The very lovely daughter of one of the men came to my home to plead with me for her father. Her plea was utterly melting, and her girlish beauty would have shaken anyone a tenth as susceptible to the sweetness of young womanhood as I am. But it meant letting them all off, not one alone, and I could only assure her that I would give it consideration. Had Churchey been present and met her, I fear he'd have promised her the freedom of her father and a letter from me to her Dad thanking him for taking the money and bestowing it upon him besides; for she was adorably beautiful and dainty and in fine taste, everything you would wish your daughter, or anyone else's daughter in your milieu, to be.

Finally one morning Churchey came to me with certain facts which had been brought to his attention by an assistant District Attorney who met him on the street and asked him to tell me and get me to phone him what I thought. It was a strange angle to the case, which if set out in fiction would be deemed just a little too implausible and unlikely to get by.

Judge Olcott confirmed the new disclosure, and put it up to me to decide upon it. One of the men accused was the son of the old Officer of the Court in which his case would be tried. The old man, who had never missed a day in Court during his forty years of service, would either have to stay home while his son faced trial, or else call that son to the bar for his offense. The melodramatic Churchey put it, "His faithful old heart would break under it, Perc."

What to do? The young man may have been less guilty than others. He might have been misled by some older person, by the casuistry of their arguments. Churchey felt that clemency was in order. Judge Olcott and I conferred with the trial Judge, who I found would welcome leniency for the sake of the old Court Officer. We all agreed to quash the whole thing. If guilty, they had already been punished much by months of strain and some imprisonment. Their game had been broken up for good. The lesson was too clear for others to imitate them.

I never regretted this unpleasant duty, nor the more pleasing action in disposing of it. But above all else, it was one more case where "my old comrade was there by my side", in the language of the popular song then current.

Churchey was again and again the old family friend in any emergency. That year my brother Ed was down with typhoid all Summer. I had the responsibility and expense of a New York house in West 88th Street, and our family, as well as my brother's illness, with two doctors daily, a day nurse and a night nurse, and two servants. Also my exacting and rushing business, the heavy mental work of studying new inventions and patenting them, the worry and strain of Ed's illness and the grave doubt that he would pull through, coupled with the illness of a sister in the mountains with my mother. Not a small shoulder-load for a boy under twenty.

Here Churchey came forward as nobly as usual. Naturally, all that Summer I remained home nights on returning from business and on Sundays and holidays. Churchey was there a great deal, ready to assist in any way with work or counsel and his invincible optimism. One hot night particularly, when hope had dimmed down, the night nurse came to us begging we would in some way locate a dog that was viciously barking and stop him, as her patient was delirious and fancied the beast was attacking him. Ed had once been bitten by a strange dog. Churchey joined me in a tour of the vicinity; we discovered the animal in a backyard of a house, where some unfeeling fellow we routed out of bed crustily declined to shut him up or take any interest in our appeal or the chance of our patient dying. I threatened the police, but Churchey brusquely told the chap he'd stop the noise or Churchey would "jolly well thrash you right here and now". A trifle old for such work, but fearless as always. He won a grudging acceptance.

Incidents minor in themselves, like the electrons that compose matter, collectively comprise the picture w which I wish to portray of the inventor of N C V steel and author of the Lost Continent of Mu, in clearer outlines than merely by verbal analysis. They make a stereographic three-dimensional relief, in place of the flat two-dimensional of just descriptive words conveying my post-mortem opinion of him, alembicated unavoidably by the mind of the narrator, or at least subject to the implication of such alembication.

There is no better place than this to refer to an important angle of this account. Not only is it pre-essential to a right judgment of Colonel Churchward's part in the discoveries about the Continent of Mu, and what I shall disclose on that matter, to know the author, the man, to comprehend his nature and his motivations, but there is more.

This is no doubt the last chance to place on record biographical facts regarding Colonel Churchward which may in time be much needed, and much missed if absent. It is not alone Today that we must consider, nor the hundreds of thousands who knew Colonel Churchward or knew of his work in his N C V steel, nor the equal or greater number that read his books. These are interested in varying extent in all that may be told of this man.

But there is also Tomorrow. Constantly the wheel of Time brings up from obscurity some genius or early pioneer in some field or other, and empty records are needle-haystacked for some facts about him to interpret his share in the invention, discovery or other matter of credit.

Churchward is already sufficiently known in Steel and in Mu to render him an appropriate subject of a complete biography of him, to make such a biography very welcome if one were available. But the future is apt to swirl him up to wider and more intensive public interest. His work in that Steel very probably will some day become the subject of especial scrutiny. What N C V steel did, and what was done to

N C V steel, must necessarily in due course of Time come into the sharp limelight. Events and the years have the habit of sinking some once famous and raising up others less so. Then everything I can supply here to give a truer, ampler picture of Colonel Churchward the man, will be of an importance not now appreciable.

I only wish I had more to set forth than I shall herein. Colonel Churchward, loquacious as to adventures and inventions, scientific and other views, was almost wholly silent upon his own private and family life, his boyhood, his childhood home, his first half of his existence. Facts about him are distinctly lacking. I feel it wise to compress this work into a very brief delineation of him as a prelude to understanding his contribution to Mu, yet I do not overlook the angles which point to completeness.

Whatever I know of him worth-while I have and will set down without reserve, except certain matters of his life confided to me and not to others, which are not relevant and not appropriate forbeeincluded, do not afford any better view of him than other facts stated here, and above all relate to persons I never met, whose side of it I had no opportunity to hear.

More than anything else in his career, his experiences in Steel, to which I now arrive, were important, of grandeur, and of tremendous effect upon himself.

His struggles in producing his alloy steel, in getting its value recognized, the secret manufacture of it, the conflict with those in Steel, litigation; his rise to opulence and a deserved pinnacle in metallurgy, his rude overthrow. What I can authoritatively tell of this will be character-illuminating, and also the sequent events which led to his publication of his Island of Mu books.

VI.

COLONEL CHURCHWARD STRAYS INTO THE JUNGLE OF STEEL

CHURCHEY'S ABSENCE IN THE WEST and abroad for a while, and a change in my business some years later, together with his removal of his residence to Mt. Vernon, temporarily diminished the frequency of our meetings.

In the interim he in conjunction with William H. Reid, organized a system and chain of lawyers throughout the United States, to act as collection factors and in all manner of law work for persons resident distant from them. It was called the Bonded List of Attorneys. These thousands of lawyers my brother Edward arranged with his Company The Fidelity & Casualty Co. of N.Y. to have bonded, so that clients were protected in dealings with such lawyers, and to eliminate from the list any unworthy of being bonded.

This brother of mine, one of the most popular insurance managers in New York until his death, was in partnership with E.E.Clapp, pioneer in Accident Insurance. The form of policy in those days was a mass of restrictions and exceptions, and illness was insured against only in a limited policy covering but a few diseases.

Clapp joined our bridge parties at times, and visited us frequently. We all had chats about the insurance, and I suggested often that they issue a full coverage against every accident and illness, to be known as "Disability Insurance". The traditions of their business were against this, companies thought more of guarding themselves against claims than of widening the scope. It was some time before they saw the light.

Clapp and my brother talked this long with me, and the older man got in the habit of coming up to lunch with me, or stopping in to ask me to finance him on one of his many real estate deals, and to urge me to throw up patents and go in with them in insurance.

At a bridge evening, Churchey added his voice quite effectively to this question. He spoke plainly to them: "Ed, every man I know says Accident Insurance is a flim-flam. I was offered a policy by one of your agents, I read it and it gave me a headache and a bellyache, but the policy didn't cover those ills, or many others. You tell them on the first page how they get it, and on the last three pages how they don't get it."

Ed and Clapp prevailed on their Company to issue this Disability Policy. I copyrighted the form for them, though it was afterward copied extensively by others. The new insurance was a decided success, and Clapp came to my house to dine, with definite proposals of partnership, insisting I must join them. I did, and spent ten years promoting Disability Insurance, through tens of thousands of agents and brokers.

Churchey strongly advised me to accept their proposition, telling me among other reasons that all inventors except himself and a few other bright souls, were "crazy cranks who will in long years make you nutty like them, while general business would give you a chance to use your talents widely."

After ten years I sold out my interests to my brother and retired from it, taking a long tour of the country and a vacation from all business for a year.

During my years in that line, Churchey had gone actively into Steel. Seeking a strong alloy for certain inventions of his in railway supplies, a lock-nut, and his tie-plate, he began to research in alloy steels. He learned there was need for a fine steel for armor plate for warships. About that time, his brother Albert gave him particulars of an alloy steel he had invented or worked out, with a very high nickel content. The Colonel [note by GTG] * World War I.

tried to get this used, but soon found it was not practical. (Parenthetically, I could disclose here a most interesting story of espionage in the World War* which came under my notice in connection with steels of high nickel content, but it isn't pertinent to our man or subject, so I shall reserve it until some day when I shall show the bold wholesale way in which our Government was bamboozled in the War and permitted and still permits foreigners of hostile nations to control much of our operations in our war and navy affairs.)

Churchey experimented and studied in various mills, made researches and talked to many people in Steel; to get in tune with "the state of the art". He spent much time in metallurgical laboratories (labor'atory he insisted on calling it, English fashion) and constantly came to me with new alloys, each of which was a world-beater. Used to his enthusiasms, I paid little attention to his stories. His claims that he was making steel in certain big mills and would soon coin millions out of it, sounded to me like his old spike and tie-plate sales contracts. But he obtained a few backers, one way or another, and organized the Churchward International Steel Corporation. Shareholders supplied him with funds to patent many of his inventions in this and foreign countries.

I was out of patents then, and very busy. I was no help to him at all. At times I loaned him small sums he needed, but looked for no return. He sought out many persons he had known to get support.

Among them my old friend Razor King Gillette, to whom I had introduced him in boyhood, who had gotten rich in bottle-stoppers and razors, and contemplated providing funds on Churchey's statements that some of the big mills whom he had shown how to make his steel, were surreptitiously infringing it, selling it to the Government. As he mentioned my name, and King knew me, and recalled my introduction of the old Colonel to him, he called on me at my office to see if I backed Churchey up.

I told him I believed Churchey a really great inventor, potentially; and his alloys, processes and electric furnaces were doubtless of a high order, but I had not investigated them at all, and could not guarantee them or the patents.

King Gillette made his own investigations, and stayed out of the Churchward Steel, not on any really debatable issue, but on a queer and irrelevant twist. After I had made Churchey $275,000 on his steel, and gotten it in use commercially besides, King berated me humorously for my tepidity at the outset, and told me why he dropped it. He had seen a letter someone gave him, signed by Churchward, saying the steel "was a communication from abroad". If so, Churchey wasn't the inventor and his patents were no good. I believe Judge Gary of U.S. Steel gave King this letter, or showed it to him. I also believe that was what led Gary to allow the Carnegie Steel Mills to infringe the patents after starting to deal with the Colonel. The fact was, of course, that this alloy "from abroad" was one of the several alloys Churchey tried and abandoned before turning his attention to the master alloy N C V, which was the subject of his patents. It was no more like Churchward steel than a thousand other alloys that hundreds of others had worked on in the past.

Guilty infringers of the Churchward Steel often claimed in defense that he was not a professional *exclusively* metallurgist, his inventions were derived from study of books, experiments of others, and deductions from those things workers in the art had done, reported and failed to do.

This I can wholly refute, because of personal direct knowledge I have that Churchey worked for years producing many steels, samples and tests of which he showed me, each being better than the last and the coming alloy for armor plates. Also because the Court records show admittedly that he had made his steel in one of the mills that afterward manufactured it.

One day Churchey came to me with a certificate for one hundred shares of his steel corporation made out to me. He insisted that I take it in part return for all the moneys I had loaned or given him in the past, including, I may add, that same day. I declined. "That, Churchey, was all in repayment to you of the cost of those hindquarters of beef, haunches of venison, saddles of South-down mutton, dozens of hams, barrels of flour and other things you carried on your broad back to our home in the blizzard of 1888 when Ed and I were children."

He had the grace to blush. "Maybe I used to lay it on thick a bit, Perc, but I don't have to about this steel; it's true gold."

"False on its face, Churchey," I replied, "and a sample of your mode of thought. A ham is a dozen turkeys if you brought it, and steel is gold just because you invented it. The only Gold in your steel is Bert Gold of Chicago." This meant Egbert H. Gold, multi-millionaire, the Railway Car Heating Czar of America, one of my best friends, whom I had christened Egbert H(eart of) Gold. A man of the rare type of firm friend and staunch supporter through thick and thin, who would battle for you and with you, play fair, trust and prove trustworthy, and accord every man credit for all he did. This last was particularly agreeable to me, since Life had shown me such a general stealing of credit from those who had said or done things, as to disgust anyone.....in the insurance business affairs everything one did or proposed on Tuesday was broadcasted by one or a dozen on Wednesday as their own achievements, and men came to me baldly and asked my admiration of their bright ideas or to confirm to others that they were the originators; While in inventions, every deviser of some machine or thing of which so little is new that it is but a "shadow of a shade " different from the others, believes that everything made or used afterwards is a rank purposed theft of his brainchild.

Bert Gold and my brother, with two others, had in my absence on a tour of the Pacific Coast, agreed to finance Churchward's suits against infringers of his steel, had tied up with some very able lawyers, advanced large sums, but made little progress.

The steel was an alloy of iron with small proportions of carbon, nickel, chromium, vanadium, manganese and other minor ingredients, and had become known to engineers as N C V steel (nickel-chrome-vanadium). Word had been passed in the steel industry and among automotive engineers, that it was a patented steel, only made by mills that would take a chance on infringing, and if used, it must be bought under confidential restrictions, called something else publicly, billed under cover, and its formula unstated. On account of its high cost, its use in commercial steels was very limited; there was no steady market for it, but it was rumored that the U.S. Government was using it.

As you can't tell such a steel from others by looking at it, as you can in most infringements of patents, the only way to prove infringement would be first to know that a given concern had used it, obtain some of that shipment, and analyse it (and if you wished to learn the maker also, trace where it came from). As Churchey remarked, "Try and do it."

All these elements had been tried in steels before and some of them used together, and all of them of course singly or in combination with still other elements. Nickel was good to harden steel, but high-nickel steel wouldn't cut or work. Chrome steel was fair; chrome-vanadium steel good for some things, poor for others. Simple vanadium-steel had been disappointing, since Swedish steels made from iron having vanadium in it had long been found good. The more vanadium you used (and it was costly) the less encouragement you got.

Churchward found that the vanadium burned or "boiled" out of the melt if you employed a high temperature, and if you didn't you failed to produce the right texture, the sought product. He proposed to use temperatures so high that he was at first laughed at, (though his lead was followed later) and he put the vanadium in the ladle near the end of the process.

He found that only by using "small proportions of each of the elements carbon, nickel, chrome, vanadium, manganese, etc." in such relations that if you increased or diminished the nickel-content you must correspondingly adjust all the others, could you produce the steel he made.

Churchward alleged that some of the large

steel mills, having learned from him and his patents, and his experiments and disclosures to them, how to make this steel, had secretly manufactured thousands of tons of it, for the United States and foreign governments, had sold it to them for armor plate for warships and other uses, and on account of the cost of the alloys and of its manufacture, were charging Uncle Sam $800 a ton instead of the $400 or $425 paid for the old steel.

The suits were at a standstill. There was a lack of any evidence that the company sued by Churchward, the great Carnegie Steel Company, had ever made any of the steel. The War and Navy departments claimed to have no knowledge of such a steel being used by them, and declined to make public the composition of the steel used in armor plates on Government warships. The Carnegie Company also alleged that the steel was not new with Colonel Churchward and that others in their plant and elsewhere had made it before; which is a common defense in most patent cases.

Before he left, Churchey had not only prevailed on me to accept his stock, but also induced me to promise to investigate his case, and see if I could inject any life into it.

My brother urged that as I had retired from the Disability business and was freer of time, I should take hold of it, as Gold and he and others had sunk so much money in it that seemed to be lost. Bert Gold also begged me to put in time on it, and others added their voices. My cousin Mac Thorburn, then Secretary of Sun Fire, bemoaned he had ever put any of his good American Scotch-hoarded dollars into such a thing, with a continuing call for more for legal expenses.

This was the beginning of my rather meteoric career in Steel. In which I very shortly came to be known to all the Executives of Steel, with entree to the sanctums of most of them. And in turn Steel came to be known to me in a manner I have never previously disclosed except privately to associates. In which I put N C V steel on the map, Colonel Churchward on the highroad to Fortune, myself in a position of temporary influence and affluence in the great Industry. Climbed not only to the Great Altitudes of Steel, but dwelt in the Inside of that queer, little-cognized Segment of Life, that Organized Aggregation of Forces, the Juggernaut of Steel (this is the way Churchey would have written it, and capitalized.) And conquering the biggest by force of law and open-handed battle and even more open-handed frankness and friendship to those that were willing; conquering the commercial resistance to the adoption of the costly high-grade N C V steel; I was in turn overthrown by the Juggernaut together with my friend Churchey, outside the breastworks.

I made a very searching investigation into this Churchward steel before connecting myself with it. I was predisposed against it because of my knowledge of old Fisherman Churchey and his propensity to enlarge his fish.

I knew, though, that there always was a fish and that he had a larger catch than others. I did not doubt that he might have a good steel, but was wary and chary about crediting his beliefs that the large mills were infringing it. As he expressed it, "had milked me dry of all I could show them, stolen my patents, tried to kill me by dumping tons of white hot steel on me, and were in cahoots with the Navy Department and fellows in there, to unload my steel on Uncle Sam at fabulous prices."

Surely no one would hesitate to distrust such a wild statement. I did, and rightly. As presented, it was not wholly true; some of it was preposterous.

But like all of Churchey's claims and discoveries, it had a firm basis in fact, if one could ferret it out to the core. Events proved that far more of it was true than I had been willing to credit, and much that even the suspicious Colonel had not visioned.

I made a very thorough examination of all the older patents, allegations of prior use etc. brought out against Churchward steel, and reports of tests of the steel. I had certain tests of it made myself under conditions exceptionally fortunate and convincing.

Evidences came before me showing that this N C V steel was not as unknown and unused as some in Steel alleged, and that Churchward was not dreaming when he claimed that many steels ostensibly older alloys were boot-leg Churchward steel masquerading or camouflaged. True that it was confined to instances where cost was no object. It was a steel handicapped by the ticket "Prohibitive cost and illegal to make on account of patents covering it"; but it was being used to some extent sub rosa. As to Governmental use, where price made no difference, I became convinced that some of the big mills had made large quantities of it and delivered them to the Navy Department despite all denials.

The patent attorneys engaged by the syndicate or Committee of backers who financed the suits, were eminent and renowned, the senior member being an old acquaintance of my patent days, who had been introduced to me by a mutual friend in his native city of Syracuse, (the inimitable Herb Perry, the original of the great fiction-character David Harum). He and his associates were experienced in steel patent litigation.

Churchey's conviction that the steel was being infringed was based quite largely upon socalled inside information coming to him from underground channels. Naturally this was not evidential and of no use in a suit. Nor did it carry much credence beyond the circle of Churchey's friends, who mostly believed in him as men did in Mohammed or Buddha, or today in Hitler and Mussolini. But as soon as he was successful in inducing me to join his fight, Churchey opened up his heart and case fully to me.

He had gotten by Masonic friendships and other means, in touch with those in Steel who knew the truth. He loved to sugar-coat this with mystery, but the patina washed off in talking to me about it. He had through European relatives, gotten so close to the elder Pierpont Morgan, that the great financier had at first introduced him to the Carnegie Steel Company, and it was understood that Carnegie was to manufacture it if found good. Just how Colonel Churchward lost his confidence no one, possibly not even Churchey himself, knew.

Churchey did not specify plainly just what foreign influences brought him to Morgan so intimately. When Judge Gary, feudal baron of Steel, asked us point-blank how he had met Morgan, my friend became Colonel Churchward of British India and replied with dignity, "I prefer that you ask that question of Morgan himself."

But I demanded facts and substance. Churchey met this challenge and brought me in contact with men in Steel who could give me those facts and did, trusting me enough to tell me what they severally knew, confident that I would not betray them; and I never did. So when I finally went into this embroglio it was with firm ground under my feet, and the ability to say to those putting up the money, that the facts were as I now conveyed to them, and that they could go forward with the certainty at least that Churchward and we were in the right. Whether we could ever establish that right and win a verdict, would be subject to the imperfect and intricate, cumbersome and absurd system of jurisprudence in patent cases as in others, which Man has built up for his own handicap in doing justice.

VII.

I WIN $275,000 FOR MY OLD FRIEND CHURCHEY

MY INVESTIGATION OF COLONEL CHUCHWARD'S case showed me he had a good fighting chance. The whole thing was in the doldrums chiefly because of the lack of coordination and the Colonel's peculiar handling of everyone concerned. His over-confident and exaggerated claims, his wild talk of getting even for the supposed attempt to dump tons of molten steel on him, which was too absurd to listen to, and his mysterious references to unnamed sources of underground information telling him what was going on in the heart of Steel, excited scepticism on the part of all, including perhaps some of the eminent Churchward Counsel. Coupled with the lack of tangible evidence supporting all these statements, they were causative of a lack of faith in his case.

His backers were quite sour at the amount of costs they had been put to, without so far any results. They did

not wish to pay any further expenses. They were appalled
at the heavy defenses offered, which flatly denied infringement, and apparently made out an impregnable case of witnesses who would testify it wasn't new with the Colonel,
previous disclosures, patents and experiments abroad and
here at home. It looked to some like a forlorn hope.

But to my mind these defenses crumbled before
full knowledge of all the facts, as frequently is the case
in patent suits, and after my investigation was completed,
I was able to supply to all the backers, who had confidence
in my business acumen, ~~with~~ enough intelligible matter to
make them agree to go further with it.

As to infringement, the regular files of the Steel
Company did not seem to contain any cards showing alloys
infringing the Churchward patents. There were white cards
and red cards and blue cards and yellow cards and other
tints of the rainbow. But one of Churchward's underground
sources of information whom he introduced to me, showed us
indubitable facts about those melts of infringing steel,
and on a preliminary hearing of testimony, the able Churchward lawyers brought out from an honest witness that there
were some salmon-pink cards. These produced, showed the
infringement and the composition of the alloys employed. The
case was proved so far as infringement went.

Meanwhile I had gotten in touch with other great
Steel interests and Executives, outside of the Carnegie Company, and learned much of the value of N C V steel, despite

its prohibitive cost, and about its random secret use and sale. I was able to show Bert Gold and other financial backers that here was not only a just suit for infringement, but a valuable steel of immense importance to American industry if the cost-factor could be modified or met.

One of the Steel insiders whom I met through the Colonel, was close to the President of the Carnegie Steel Company, Alva C. Dinkey, one of the really great men of Steel. He proposed that I permit him to introduce me to Dinkey, and effect a meeting. But this was done in such a manner that I doubted the propriety of it, and did not follow it at that time, though he intimated that Dinkey wanted to meet me. I left it an open question.

The suit now became very much alive, we pressed our case forcefully. The big Steel interests engaged experts in steels to swear to all manner of prior uses or attempts to produce this steel. Our facts, and the skilled cross-examination by our eminent Counsel, who were among the best in America, slashed these claims to pieces, Dr. John A. Matthews, afterwards made President of the great Crucible Steel Company, told me of his activities in it. He had experimented to produce just such a steel as Colonel Churchward had, but failed to make a successful "melt" . Tests showing it a rather miserable piece of metallurgical production, he abandoned it. "Had I kept on, and had faith in it, and produced a successful melt, I might have been the inventor of N C V steel, instead of a witness testifying against Colonel

Churchward's patents." But Matthews was too square to try to make himself out the inventor because he had made one abortive attempt to reach the goal the Colonel had worked so many years to attain. Instead, he agreed to cooperate with me to advance the manufacture and use of this very valuable steel, with full credit to Churchward, and only the intervention of other people prevented this from finally eventuating; Steel, Inside Steel, is a queer animal, of which those who hear the truth and don't encounter it personally as I did, are prone to say "Nonsense! There just ain't no sich animile".

Other steel men were not so retiring. But they achieved nothing in the way of defeating that Carnegie suit. One expert was a man who became famous as the "coloratura steel expert". It seems he had seen a melt of steel years before and knew what was in it by the color of the molten metals of the alloy. He could judge temperatures by colors of course, also. So it was easy for him to tell just what ingredients were in any melt of alloy steel. On cross-examination by the dignified Patent Counsel, who was posted, this expert admitted that in fact he was, on some official license examination or other, found to be rather "colorblind", which I believe was an inherent and permanent characteristic. It detracted somewhat from his authority as a color expert on molten metals.

The Steel people carried the suit abroad, and we had to send Counsel to Europe to meet this attack. Our foes combed England and the Continent to find experts who would testify that they had made this steel, or that it was not an invention to make it, as anyone could have thought it out. But the great French Steel expert Guillot would only say, (for $1500 of American steel money) that while it might have been possible for a man like him to have invented it, he didn't think ordinary steel men could have.

The eminent Sir Richard Hadfield declined to help them one jot. He stated that he considered N C V steel a fine and valuable product of Colonel Churchward's genius. Hadfield knew how little changes in steel alloys make wide and astonishing differences in the product. His celebrated Hadfield steel was an instance. Manganese had been used in steel for decades. Up to two percent, the more you used, the better the steel. But beyond two or three percent it weakened the steel, made it worse and worse as you increased the dose. Hadfield tried using a very much higher percentage to see how bad it got, and to his surprise found that when you get in about twelve percent of manganese, you produce a steel so strong that it has long been used for bank vaults and safes to an enormous extent. Just opposite to what everyone expected. A lesson in steel in itself.

They did prove that a similar steel to Churchward's had been made in the Krupp works in Germany, but I had information that this had been done only after Colonel Churchward had filed a German patent application, and that it was the custom in the German Patent Office at that time to have Krupp scrutinize all war materials inventions that came to the Patent Office.

Finally, in regular conventional fashion, came an open invitation from the Carnegie Steel Company for its Counsel to meet us and our Counsel and see if we could settle the case. Churchey, through his underground channels, was informed that they wished to meet me, and try to prevail upon us to accept some small sum, knowing that the Colonel was "on his uppers" and his backers none too confident. Further, that they would expect the patent to be turned over to them.

I confess that I doubted if all this would turn out to be accurate, but it did, to the last item, except that they expected the control only of the Governmental war materials part of the steel, and not interfere with what I was doing to promote it commercially, which they didn't believe would come to anything on account of the cost. Churchey's sources of information were always so veiled in mystery and secrecy as to seduce the credulous but repel the practical sceptical man of affairs perhaps wrongly. Most of them could never be checked up. But where I had such opportunity, I found them substantially justified, provided the facts had been given to me in Churchey's serious quiet manner, free of braggadocia and bombast, which were always adequate trade mark of unreliability.

We accepted this olive branch and I agreed to go, provided Bert Gold joined me, and that we have full power to make a deal or reject one, on the spot. Also that all factions unite in naming a sum of money which we were to make our initial proposition.

A meeting was held, of all Churchward backers and large shareholders, with the Colonel, Counsel, and myself. All minds met in stating this sum as $500,000 for full release, and patent rights if required. (Of course, only the patents for this steel; Churchward had several others, not all steels,...an electric furnace, a pyrometer, etc.)

No one had invited the Colonel to be there, and all the backers vetoed his going. I would have taken him willingly, but he rather stood on his dignity and showed no wish to come.

Our conference with the enemy was held in the Marlborough-Blenheim at Atlantic City, and lasted all day. The Patent Counsel **of** the United States Steel Corporation and the Carnegie Company, Charles C. Linthicum, made a two hour speech. A masterly presentation of the case against the patents. He showed that before Churchward, the Steel art was developing countless alloys. It was a matter of metallurgical skill, trial and error, and not much invention to it. Along came King James (as he affectionately called Colonel Churchward, whom he knew and genuinely liked as a fisherman and in every way except as a metallurgist) stole everybody's thunder and crashed into Steel, where he didn't belong. They could wipe out all shadow of claim that Churchward invented anything, this chance melt of steel was more or less known all along to everyone, but it just hadn't been used, until, as steel technique improved, they finally made something out of it. He liked old King James, he loved his fish stories and his visions of grandeur and conspiracies, and he was prepared to pay $25,000 instead of going ahead and busting our patents as we must see he had done already. He would take an exclusive license for armor plate and other war materials, leaving us the rest, as he knew I had dreams of doing something with it in the commercial field, and they knew there was nothing in that.

My associates had arranged that I would carry the burden of our side. I offered Bert Gold the floor first. He declined in an aside to me: "I think they've got old Churchey smashed. I'd give 'em the release, the license, the whole patent, the stock in the Company and Churchey's whiskers for the $25,000, and get out. It's a flop."

But luckily my answer to the Steel Trust Counsel seemed to throw a bombshell into the conference. In brief, ~~shortly~~ it was this:

N C V Steel has been proved by tests known to me, and others under my direction, to have a tensile strength of 125,000 pounds to the square inch. There is no known steel in the world that approaches this except Sir Richard Hadfield's super-manganese steel, which has 160,000 pounds, but is not usable for such purposes as N C V as we all know, and not capable of doing what N C V does in armor plate and other forms. Before Churchward, no one knew how to make it, and no one had. **of others** Failures to make a successful melt of the steel do not defeat an inventor's patents, but prove that he succeeded in producing a great invention where others had been unable to. Their own expert, Dr. John A. Matthews admitted to me freely that he had tried and failed. Colonel Churchward had from time to time shown me for years his better and better steels, and I knew he had worked on it long before any of the socalled experts had even tried it. He had been in their mills, his ideas had become hazily known to them. They sought to do it without him, and when they couldn't, they had copied his methods, his plans, and had learned from this "outsider", this "upstart", this intruder into the inner sacred sanctum of Steel, just what to do, what to use, and how to make this steel.

Churchward had shown them that only by using certain small quantities of all these ingredients in certain proportions had success been possible. If you used a high carbon steel, you produced another product altogether, whatever else you added to it. Too much nickel, too much chrome, you went astray. Besides, that called for more vanadium, and apart from the great cost of ferro-vanadium, it was too rich and you had a useless melt. The Colonel had shown that you must use higher temperatures in the furnace, they were no doubt using his high temperature patent though they denied it. He had demonstrated that you must put the vanadium in the ladle toward the end, or you lost its chief value.

I pointed out that Steel had even altered its after-manufacture heat treatments through what Churchward had taught them. I revealed that I knew they had so strongly boasted and boosted the unique value of this N C V steel of Churchward's to the United States Government that they had secured a price of $800 a ton for it from our Navy Department instead of the $400 a ton previously paid for the old steel.

That I knew the ballistic tests it had withstood, the tests of its tensile strength made by the Navy Depart‑
That Churchward Steel on warships was salt-waterproof.
ment and the Steel Corporation's own forces too. I told him we knew the dates they had made this Steel and sold it to the Government and the total amount of sales. Twenty million dollars' worth of Churchward Steel to Uncle Sam alone. On this we were entitled to all their profits if we could maintain our patents in Court. They had brought twenty Steel men to swear against Colonel Churchward's valuable invention, yes; but here were twenty million witnesses for us....... twenty million gold dollars declaiming in the convincing language which only money talks, that this was one of the most priceless inventions Steel had ever known. Their offer of $25,000 was nothing I could even discuss, and unless they invited me to name a dignified sum in settlement, which would be commensurate with the importance of our subject but modest in comparison with the gross sales of $20,600,000.....all was off.

From that moment there was little doubt in my mind that I had won Colonel Churchward his claim and that these people would settle. Lawyer Linthicum lost completely his aura of confidence, and got in touch with Pittsburgh on the phone.

Many of those who knew of my final settlement with the Carnegie Company thought I must have "put the screws on 'em hard ", "pulled something big out of my sleeve" and so forth. None of this has ever been in my line. Nor would it have been at all effective with such men, who were no children. What was required was a convincing picture of Churchward's side of the case in such terms as simultaneously to open their eyes to the right, and the weight of our attack, to replace the complacent, patronizing image of the Colonel as an interloper in Steel who had done nothing, and so to chop their defenses into mincemeat that they would regard the opportunity to settle now as something not lightly to be passed by.

After luncheon, on request, I was invited to name our price. I offered to settle for $500,000. We spent the afternoon in debate, and now the dominance of the conference had shifted to our side. At one point Linthicum appealed to Bert Gold. "It's too big a sum, and you know it, Gold. It's ten times what we'll pay. " Bert answered, between puffs of his cigar, "Yes, it is big, Linthicum, but after hearing Percy Griffith this morning.....you'll pay it, Linthicum, you'll pay it."

Our $500,000 was rejected and no counter-offer made. Churchey was downcast. He and others felt I should have nursed them up to some fair figure and closed with them. I reminded Churchey that his own information had told him the lawyer would only come authorized to offer a small sum. He could not have closed for an amount more than his limit. If his phone to Pittsburgh had not secured another offer, it was because they thought they could screw us down to their own.

Churchey bemoaned the lost opportunity. " All I wanted was to get some money out, buy a farm, settle on it, and spend all my time on the work I'm doing on the Island of Mu problem. Perc, I wish I could drop all this and go to Yucatan. I'd get close to the secret of Mu, and show up a lot of people who think they know so much about Yucatan and the Mayans."

"Like old Le Plongeon did. But wait a bit, Churchey", I told him, " One meeting isn't all to these shrewd Steel men. I'm not certain it's dead yet."

But the old Colonel talked Mu with me for hours, and seemed to have lost hope for anything out of Steel. He had dreamed of my coming back with a bag of gold from Atlantic City, and our both going to Yucatan to delve in the Mayan mysteries and solve all the problems of Mu.

While the case was dragging, with long waits in between, and while testimony was being taken abroad, I was working on the plans to build up the steel in the market, but Churchey was dreaming of Mu and resolving how to spend the Steel Trust's moneys in archaeology and research and in running a farm on the borders of a fine fishing-ground somewhere near.

All this I had strangled by not seizing my opportunity, when I had the genial Linthicum "pretty well buffaloed", to pin him down to some sum, no matter what, take it, and put the Colonel in a position to divert his brains to the greater issue of where was Mu and what had happened to it..... and also fish all day or in betweentimes.

Two months later came a definite personal invitation from Alva Dinkey, President of the Carnegie Steel Compnay asking me to meet him and see if we could not arrive at some settlement. Again Churchey's informant told us they would make us a small offer of fifty thousand dollars and endeavor to hold us down to it.

I accepted this invitation, with Bert Gold and Counsel as before. I called a Churchward meeting and all unanimously resolved that I should use my judgment on the spot, and above all, take what we could get.

From the moment I met Alva Dinkey I liked him. and in the years of our acquaintance liked him more. Frankly, I have always been obliged to make allowance for most business men of no philosophic or scientific or cosmic or sympathetic economical and ethical viewpoint. My gods are not their gods, nor their set narrow limits and horizon mine. I have always gazed with deep pity on the too-fat or too-scrawny, out-of-condition-bodies, sallow or purple faces, starved or petrified minds, the protruding bellies, the pompous poise, the

drooped shoulders, the form bearing a vanished semblance
of athletic, leaping, singing, light-hearted man, now much
like the shell cast off by a locust, or a puffed-out fungus-
shot ear of corn. The intellect which has been compressed
and shrunken into the shape of a mere business machine, a
robot of routine, with no earnest seeking consciousness of
the real underlying nature of matter, motion, mind and man,
their and his future in the cosmos.

But recognizing that there are few Newtons and
Spencers, Faradays and Rutherfords, Edisons and Marconis,
Shapleys and Eddingtons, Jeans and Huxleys, Haeckels, Humboldts,
Curies, Kelvins, Comptons, Millikans, I appraise business men
according to the standards of the world in which they move.
You do not appraise an office building or apartment as a place
of personal residence for your own self which craves the
simple quiet peace of a flower-studded, vine-clad home; but
in and for its function and purpose as a building of that
class.

There have been many men in life, and some in Steel,
who have within the standards and limits of their milieu,
measured up to great heights as men, as persons of worth and
integrity, charm and loyalty, square-shooting and square-think-
ing. To my friend Bert Gold, richer in friendship than
in his millions, I added Alva Dinkey.

He knew Steel, worked in it most of his life. He
had a wide grasp of affairs. He won the confidence of men
in a moment and held it for a half-century. Invariable, dependable, admired, liked, loved in all the corridors and cran-

nies, the offices and mills of Steel.

President Dinkey opened up our conference in bluff hearty style. He cast aside all defenses. His lawyers said they could beat us. He didn't care, he'd concede that ours could lick hell out of his. That our inventor was a genius and all their Steel men just has-beens. That we could sail in and get a verdict. But the facts were...
...... Here Dinkey rolled off figures and statistics, price sheets, accountants' statements, and all the technical jargon and details of Steel, to show that they had laid out so much money in this steel, that there wasn't a cent of profit in it, he had suffered a heavy loss on it all. If there had been any money in it, we could get it in Court, or he'd gladly give us some of it. But there were the figures; cards on the table. We were all fighting over spoils that didn't exist. Playing our hands with infinite skill, (he bowed to the lawyers) in a game where there wasn't a cent of stakes in the pot. This, which took some time to outline, was a tough hurdle.

I had through my friend and associate George F. Seward, President of The Fidelity & Casualty Co., and former Minister to China, met and known Andrew Carnegie, founder of the Carnegie Steel Co., and the U.S. Steel Corporation. He was fond of saying with a Scotch twinkle and a Scotch burr, that there were more ways of computing cost in the Steel trade than of killing a cat. And I had met

Mark Twain and had heard him tell an apochryphal story which afterward went the rounds.

So I first told this story to Dinkey, now quite old: Twain went into a book-shop to buy a book. "I claim 40% discount because I am an author, another 40% because I am unhappily a publisher too. Then as a librarian, as I have stocked so many of my friends' with books borrowed from me. Then the religious discount to clergymen, as my father or uncle ...." The dealer wrapped up the book. "Tell me how much I owe you, Mr. Clemens, and I will pay it."

I told Dinkey, "In all these sheets of figures you omit one that computes just how much the Churchward Company owes you for damages for your infringement. Your accountants could prepare for you sheets showing, with Linthicum's aid, how much the Courts will assess us, the owners of the patents, as damages to be paid you because of your loss through your infringement of our patents." Dinkey laughed heartily. I quoted him his own founder, Andrew Carnegie, about ways of computing costs. Then I ripped up the web of figures. " You got $800 a ton for steel you used to sell for $400. The cost of what you added was not $100 a ton, so you made $300 more than you used to make per ton, and that was always good money, as you know. But the whole cost of all the materials was how much, all told? What was the actual cost of making it? How many days of a furnace? How many days' labor of men? What is the cost per day of a furnace in all Steel mills averaged? How much overhead can you work in?

You can't charge interest on Carnegie's $400,000,000 of bonds. When you come to an accounting of profits on this $20,000,000 of gross sales, it is not your servile accountants that will make up the figures, but the Master appointed by the Federal Court."

Dinkey took Linthicum aside to confer. My associates beamed and whispered to me, "They're going to raise that offer they were set to make us, from $50,000 to....."

They offered us $150,000. We refused and clung to our $500,000, offering to "shade it" but not depart greatly from it. Here our Counsel made the only criticism either of my loyal allies offered in both our meetings: "For God's sake, Griffith, if you use that phrase 'shade it' once more I'll die, and Dinkey winces every time you hurl it at him. Try a synonym for a change."

From 9 A.M. to 4 P.M. again we jockeyed and dickered. We finally agreed on a settlement of $275,000 for full release on infringement and exclusive license for war materials. We had stuck at $250,000 offered by them, and $300,000 nominated by us, at a deadlock until our brilliant Counsel, by a tactful and winning speech, effected the compromise and won us that last $25,000.

What could we have gotten if we had won the suit? No one knows. Would they have beaten us? No one could hope to tell then. We were elated. Bert Gold congratulated me on this big stroke for the Churchward interests. All the stockholders and backers of Churchward now had their money back with a big profit. There were still more infringers to sue and deal with. There was the commercial end of the Steel, which now that Carnegie, the great U.S. Steel Corporation, had recognized the patents as valid, I might be able to make the means of earning millions, if I could overcome the cost obstacles.

"Besides, Perc, you've gotten justice for your old boyhood friend Churchey, put him above want, and as you like the old scrapper, this probably means a lot to you to have accomplished. It's been a close call for Churchey. I didn't think he or we would ever get a damn cent out of it."

And Alva Dinkey and I had started a friendship which endured for years, despite later events which might have strained it to the breaking point, despite that Steel placed the great-hearted Alva Dinkey on the spot later, in a position alike difficult and undeserved.

VIII.

ADVENTURES IN STEEL --

BRIGHT HOPES FOR CHURCHWARD

WE PHONED OUR LAWYERS' OFFICE IN NEW YORK to convey the glad tidings to Churchey and his backers, of the victory. Gold went back to Chicago, promising to meet me in a few days again East and plan what we would do to profit by this big opportunity to push the commercial sale of N C V steel, and get after the other infringers.

I returned to New York, pardonably ready to accept a small celebration of our conquest of the Steel Trust, and opening up the pathway to the promised land.

Somewhat of a disillusionment was substituted. Churchey, phoned the news at his Mt. Vernon home, reacted unexpectedly. These Steel men, after fighting him for years, had surrendered and paid up? Had actually handed us the enormous sum of $275,000? Then that showed they were frightened out of their boots, and if rightly handled, would certainly have disgorged millions. The whole thing had been botched and mismanaged. If only he'd had someone who would really fight for him, slay the dragon, and bring home those millions! If he had himself been there to give a tinge of the old Army days to the battle. There had been too much pussyfooting with these rich Steel men all along. What had been needed was fire and brimstone, loud talk, a big howl and scrap, wholesale denunciations, and the ill-gotten spoils of the infringers fairly wrested from their trembling clutch.

He rushed down to the City to see my brother and bewail our ill-luck, his loss of a fortune, and my gross incompetency. Why hadn't I won him two million dollars? If these wealthy Steel magnates had decided to settle, and had paid over this stupendous sum of $275,000, they would just as easily have been made to pay a million, two million, three, or more. Call it two, to be moderate !

My brother Ed, busy with insurance, overcome by the Colonel's eloquence, condoled with him, and agreed we should have tapped the Trust for bigger money. In Court we could have collected more, if we had won, and if we had been able to show higher profits. What a piking sum it was, after all, $275,000 ! Even one million might have been creditable, though two were better, of course, but a paltry $275,000 ! It was pitiable. Nothing that our Counsel could say in extenuation moved either of them. It had been a flop. I should have had more guts and blood and iron and pounding with my fists on the table. Churchey depicted a correct scene, as he would have played it, with himself in the role of Napoleon in the palace of the Austrian Emperor, seizing a valuable and precious vase, dashing it to the ground in fragments and crying out dramatically, "There's my terms, take 'em or leave 'em, and if you refuse I'll smash you all as I've just smashed that vase !"

When I was greeted with this view of the matter, over the phone, I consigned Churchey and his Steel to the very nadir of the nethermost, and repaired to my home at Stamford. I washed my hands of Steel.

Bert Gold wired me from Chicago to meet him in New York for breakfast. I did. He was wrathy with Churchey and sour at Ed. He called my brother in, and minced no words, either about the Colonel or anything else.

"Why, damn his eyes, has he gone stark staring mad and you with him? You and I and Churchey and the whole crew asked Perc two months ago to go to Atlantic City and make them an offer of $500,000. Then how the hell could he get us $2,000,000 ? Then two weeks ago, when this last meeting was set at Philadelphia, everyone asked him to go there and close it up, for the most he could get of that sum we had fixed. Just how did your wild friend Churchey expect him to drag down $2,000,000 out of $500,000 ? Are you crazy, you and Churchey, or do you think I'm a damn fool? Were any of you there? Well, I was. When I came back from Atlantic City, I told you it was a tough case, they had a strong set-up and might beat us. After their lawyer punctured old Churchey's claims, I'd have given them the release, the patents, and the Company and Churchey's whiskers, as I told Perc, taken the $25,000 and marked it off as a fizzle. But Perc had just the right things to say and shook them up a bit, Then Alva Dinkey showed ground for beating us on any heavy damages, and again Perc pulled it out of the fire. He worked hard to squeeze that $275,000 out of them, and both our lawyer and I were in touch with it as we went along, and approved everything he said and did. It's the only money Churchey ever got out of his damned steel, and as Perc here has quit it in disgust, I say it's likely all he ever will get out of it."

My brother Ed was unique in being one man who always admitted he was wrong quickly and positively. Time and again he would impulsively jump one way in business, to find it bad, (as who doesn't?) but the instant it so turned out, no one had to wait to hear of it, he came himself to show you what had eventuated,

"You're right, Bert !" he now said. " I think I let Churchey feel I agreed with him. I forgot we'd ourselves made that offer of $500,000 two months ago. I'll get hold of Churchey and tell him he's all wet. I can handle him."

But while he could handle a Churchey down in the world, and leaning on his backers, no one, not even Ed, could control a Churchey who had suddenly become possessed of riches. He ran amok, in many ways. He bewailed the fact that he had ever organized a Company. Why couldn't he have kept the patents and now had all this money to himself? His various friends and persons he had lassoed into buying stock in it, owned just short of half the stock. There were legal expenses of about $30,000 to pay, and repay those who had advanced them, together with the share due them for risking that money.

Then there was ten percent due me by our agreements, I had never asked Churchey to put that in writing. I'd as soon have slapped my old chum in the face. We all knew of it, no one dreamed he'd go back on it.

But Churchey, with all this money, was a different man. He was never the kind, like Ed, to find himself wrong and come tell you so. He was always right. I may instance an occasion showing this, and something of his mental trend. Discussing some of his patented alloys using titanium, he called it a "rare metal, like vanadium". I told him there was double the amount of titanium in the earth, as of carbon. He blew up. "You're daffy! You forget all the coal mines, petroleum, everything." He would refute me later; meanwhile he warned all present not to credit such a thing. At the same meeting, he asked me whether he wasn't right in a quarrel with a Cornell professor, who pronounced an extinct saurian "diplod'ocus " while Churchey pronounced it "diplodo'cus". I told him he was correct as to the genus diplodocidae, but as to the only animal in that genus, the diplodocus, the professor was right in saying "diplod'ocus".

A week later he wrote me from Washington:"By the way, talking to Dr.Walcott today, about titanium volume,he said you were wrong about there being many times as much carbon as titanium; there is about twice as much titanium only. And he also said you and I were both wrong about "diplodo'cus", it is "diplod'ocus" "!

In this $275,000 matter, Churchey was a mule. I had wrecked his chances of a fortune, and lost him the millions he should have had. As for my ten percent, he thought that would only be if I got him a million or more dollars; he had never agreed to pay me ten percent for selling him out to the Steel magnates for such a piffling sum as this $275,000.

When I met him at the Company meeting, made my report to the stockholders, shook hands with the score of grateful men and women who congratulated and thanked me, I declined to debate it with him. I simply shook the dust of Churchward Steel off my feet, and told my old friend he didn't need me any more, he now had enough for his comfort for the rest of life, so Godspeed.

But Bert Gold was of a different fibre. He was shocked, damned Churchey, damned everybody, and declined to listen to such an ending. He told the Colonel, "Churchey, if it hadn't been for Percy Griffith, you'd be rolling in the gutter today. You make me ashamed to be in the same Company with you. And how do you expect to make any money out of your steel commercially without him? Who's to charm the money out of the other infringers? You? Ed? Me? The lawyers? Wake up, you've thrown away your big chance, Churchey, and you go right out to Stamford and tell Perc you've been a damned ingrate and a fool as well."

Gold phoned me he would renounce his share of the settlement as a backer, take back his advances paid, and turn over the rest to me. This I of course declined, wholly or in part. Needless to say, it was just the characteristic "pure Gold" of the man. It was his way. Square and loyal, abhorring bad sportsmanship. Trusting to one he knew played fair with him. (So, parenthetically, was John W. Gates of the Steel magnate gallery, who once when I was entertaining some friends at dinner in Saratoga, came up to speak to one of my guests. "I'm going out on a party, Jim, and I don't want to carry this roll; keep it for me." My guest wished to count it before him, but Gates laughed and left. We counted the money at Jim's request; it was $387,000.)

Finally Gold arranged a compromise whereby the Company and the Committee of backers jointly paid me $12,000 of the $27,500 due me. Dividends on my stock added some $3000 to this.

Churchey, as his share, received from dividends on his stock, about $135,000. He proceeded to build himself a country estate at Lakewood, Connecticut, where he had ten acres and a cow, could fish all day, experiment, work on the Island of Mu all night, and indulge in various researches. Bought a car, learned to drive it, despite his age.

I was free of steel, and intended to remain so. Churchey wrote me asking my opinion on a scientific matter, and I tore up the letter. Then he phoned me in panic. No one had thought, he said, to deduct income taxes from the $275,000 before paying it out, and now the Government was going to arrest him and other officers of the Company for not reporting the income and paying some awfully heavy sum and penalties. I told him to take it up with those who were handling his affairs, I wasn't an officer and never had been, and hung up. Others called me for help, however, so I took up this matter, analysed it for the Internal Revenue Bureau as follows:

> The Patents were worth millions. A license we gave in settlement was worth more than $275,000. We had settled a suit for damages of more than a million, by accepting this compromise. Therefore $275,000 was a settlement for less than the amount of our claim. Therefore we had parted with assets of more than $275,000 and it represented a loss, not a gain. If the Bureau couldn't see it, I hoped they'd talk to Churchey, who could show them I'd lost him millions, or to Dinkey, who could make figures sit up and dance for him.

The Income Tax Bureau Solomonically decided that of the moneys received, $250,000 was assets cashed in, not income, the other $25,000 was income and must pay a tax and penalties; but as legal costs had been $30,000, there was a loss for the year of $5000 and no tax, no penalties, no jails or arrests.

I may say here that in all corporation, estate or other matters I have been associated with, I have on all questions arising about income taxes, insisted upon the matters being taken to the Tax Bureau in advance, the full problem stated with all facts and figures, and the Department asked to say what they wished done about it. Thrash it out then and there, and report it as agreed. If a certain banker who stood trial in criminal court on an income tax charge, had taken the question up beforehand with the Bureau, I believe they would have discussed and suggested the very step in registering losses for which he was indicted, and there would have been no possible prosecution. If not, they would have outlined just what they would require and he could just as easily have so done it. (Please, Mr. Critic, don't tell me this has nothing to do with Churchward, his Steel and his Mu; I know that, but some reader, even you yourself, may profit by it more than Churchey got out of both these pet hobbies of his.)

    N C V steel made no progress. Stockholders and backers came to me discouraged. "Suits against other infringers are at a standstill. No one can get anyone to manufacture it. Nothing is done except hold meetings at which Churchey scraps with everyone." This condition continued for some time.

    Then one day Churchey appeared at my house in Stamford, quite cool, friendly and unruffled, as though nothing at all had ever happened between us. Chatted and joked, played with my children, stayed to luncheon, talked science, geology, ethnology. Asia, the Mayans in Yucatan, their progress through the rest of the globe, and Mu. He showed me a schedule or chart he had drawn up, proving that the names of the letters of the Greek alphabet were themselves Mayan words, which when read in correct order, were a description of the flood which had destroyed the Island of Mu, and this record of that flood was the origin of the Biblical story of Noah as well.

"I recall something of that in old Le Plongeon's stories, Churchey," I replied. "No," he answered, "I got this from a tablet I saw in India, in Mayan, which a priest showed me." "Nonsense, Churchey" I said, "you can't read Mayan, and you never told me of any tablet at any time. But if you read it, then why spring it on me as a new thing of your own?" He answered, meekly, "I didn't. All my knowledge of Mu came from esoteric and Oriental sources, in Asia, in Oceania, and I couldn't have originated them myself, could I, if they were genuine? Besides, Le Plongeon's was different."

In the afternoon he demanded of me why I had deserted an old friend and left him at the mercy of the Steel Juggernaut. He confirmed that no headway was being made, insisted that everyone in the Churchward Company and in Steel was trying to gyp and rook him. Things were in a dreadful state.

"Why, you old barefaced rogue and villain, you", I replied lightly. "You Scrooge and Uriah Heep and trebly damned ingrate. How do you expect me to bother with your wretched steel when you repaid my two years' work with such mean, dirty, and thoroughly crooked grand larceny?"

"Now hold on, Perc. That was just my way of getting the backers to pitch in and pay part of your dues. Also

I had to placate a lot of the fellows I'd made promises to, who would have thought I should pay your part out of my own share, instead of the Company paying it, whereas I only got $135,000 out of it as majority stockholder. But at last I got you $12,000, didn't I? It wasn't right for all you did, but you and I have always been friends, Perc......"

"Yes, I've always been Perc to you, Churchey. Perc ! You mean 'purse' ! A pocketbook you could tap any minute since I made money as a boy of sixteen. " I went to a desk and took out a blank deposit slip with some pencil marks on it. "Do you remember, two years ago, when you had three teeth left, couldn't eat or talk more than a mumble, and I gave you $250 for a set of false teeth? Well, read what you wrote there then."

He blushed as he read: "Some day....$250 paid back..... thousands given me by P.T.G. paid back.... and $200,000 besides.... Happy day! "

"But I will, sooner or later, Perc. You just wait." You couldn't argue with Churchey. You either kicked him out or laughed and played ball with him. Neither you, nor the world, nor himself, could make him over. He must be accepted or rejected as is.

I rejected. "No, thanks, **Churchey**, I'm not biting on painted spoons today. I'm out."

The old man broke down and wept, to my great distress. He begged me to forgive him. "I was distraught.

When I got that money in from you, I went loco. I got ideas that I could have dragged millions out of them. But now nothing comes, nothing breaks for us. No one ever got me a cent out of anything, except you. You must help me again. I'll sign any papers you want, power of attorney, proxy on all my stock, exclusive selling agency for the United States......"

But I was obdurate. I didn't care to mix in with it. I had met Steel men supposed to be robbers, to save an innocent friend from their rapacity. They had been men of honor and fairness, had played the game with me honestly. The man I was to save from their injustice had been himself Injustice personified, and a prize ingrate. I was distinctly fed up.

Churchey, however, continued his campaign to win me back. Here a strange event intervened to help him, and to give him a chance to offset his meanness to me. A former business associate had rather improperly calculated the accounts of our dealings and my receipts were $26,500 short of what was owing. Years passed, and he wished to refund this sum withheld from me, but in some way that would "save his face ". So, knowing the Churchward stock would likely pay well, he proposed to me that he should repay me "that $20,000," he called it, by buying my stock in the Company. I declined. He asked Colonel Churchward to persuade me. Churchey came to me, urged me to take the $20,000, and he would give me from his own stock another one hundred shares so I would still own the same amount as before. "This will also set me straight with you, Perc, and pay you the money I chiseled out of you on the Carnegie deal."

As such a transfer of a hundred shares to me would have left Churchey with less than a majority of the stock, and lost him voting control except with the votes of myself or other shareholders, the generosity of this offer is obvious, and in direct contrast to his acts and attitude when I won him the $275,000.

I of course could not consider such a thing, no matter what balance he owed me, but I conveyed my stock to the debtor who wished to repay my $26,500 by this peculiar roundabout method.

Naturally, after such a magnificent gesture by the old man, I could no longer refuse to aid him on his steel, and again took hold of it, and sought to repair the damage done. Things were in bad shape. The suit filed against the chief infringer outside of Carnegie Company, had been wofully balled up by Churchey himself.

In referring to this suit, I might easily employ the true name of the infringer (Bethlehem Steel), since I do not allege in any of the long action, that the infringer did anything wrongful, as judged by common business rules and the routine of litigation. But if nobody did wrong, then the Law was at fault, for the Colonel and his Company did not in my opinion get justice.

So I shall call this infringing Steel the Biggs

Steel Corporation, because it was the biggest user of the Churchward Steel after Carnegie. I do this because there might be some who would attribute wrongdoing in some way to this concern, in spite of my disclaimer, and I have no desire to cause discomfort to anyone in that company, or any stockholder owning shares in it. The purpose of this work is to do justice to some, and to the facts, but in no case to do harm to anyone, justly or otherwise. I used the correct name of Carnegie Company because there was no even seeming ground for anyone misjudging them, or harshly judging them; their infringement they settled for.

    My brother Ed introduced Churchey to the Vice President of a Bank which handled accounts of the Biggs Mill. Supposedly a friend of Ed's, this banker told the Colonel that Biggs had never made any of his steel, but had bought it all from Carnegie, made it into plates and sold it to the Government. As we had settled with Carnegie, that steel was covered in our deal with Dinkey. It hadn't occurred to Ed or Churchey to doubt this, or to ask me to see Dinkey and get the truth. Churchey met an official of Biggs and offered to settle our suit for the nominal sum of $25,000.

    My first step was to go to Dinkey and ask him. He was in a tight position. Steel ethics is hidebound. Steel must stand with Steel in such fights. Still, he and I had become friends, and he wished to play fair with me.

If our suit came to trial, he would be expected to back up
Biggs. Yet I would also expect him to tell the truth. A
nice pickle for Dinkey. I left with the idea that Biggs
had not bought all its N C V from Carnegie. Officially I
was referred to Ray C.Bolling, General Counsel of the Steel
Trust, socalled, and I believe, brother to Mrs.Woodrow
Wilson.

Bolling was on the eve of departure for France,
where he was the first American officer killed. Traveling
in his car through the lines, his chauffeur missed the way
and they were surrounded by Germans. Too plucky to surrender, Bolling ordered his chauffeur to a shell-hole, and with
an automatic revolver undertook to fight a company of German soldiers. A fine specimen of man, about thirty five, a
good horseman, we talked horses and my then recent disclosure
of why the Kaiser clique had dragged America into the war,
which he assured me Wilson agreed with, and years after I
learned from authority was also known to Clemenceau and
others. Some time I shall further reveal all that followed
from that disclosure, but not here.

Colonel Bolling also told me that he and Wilson
believed our entrance into the war marked its end, and that
its final outcome would be a World Confederation and the
elimination of all wars from earth. Could he be here now!
And Wilson. And Tigre Georges, who thought he had cloven
Germany in half for keeps. Turning to Steel, Bolling ex-

plained that he could not admit that any of Biggs' sales of Churchward steel had been made by them, nor would he claim Carnegie had sold them all they used. I could draw my own conclusions from this. I did. He advised me strongly to settle with Biggs. "You don't know what you're up against. It's not just issues you can see and anticipate. Griffith, don't take your goose to the slaughter!"

"But, Bolling, it's your goose as well as mine. Your people bought the exclusive right for war materials. If Biggs wins, you lose all your patent rights in this steel."

Bolling was embarrassed. He intimated that there were things he couldn't speak of. I learned later what they were. Startling things. Things that were unjust and unusual, and eventually smashed Colonel Churchward and Churchward steel. I shall reveal them shortly, to the surprise of all those who follow the fortunes of old genius and fisherman Churchey, and his career climaxing in the work on Mu. To the astonishment of many that such things could be done, that Steel does or has done these things to anyone, that Law and the Courts do these things or allow them.

In any case Bolling made it clear that the ethics of Steel required Carnegie to stand by Biggs, happen what may. He ended our chat on a very true prophecy: "Maybe I won't be here to have to witness the slaughter, Griffith."

When I reported back what I had discovered, Churchey was furious at the banker who had misled him. I attended the next meeting with Biggs Company, met a Vice President who was appointed to settle with us, but he had no authority beyond the $25,000 the Colonel had named. He conceded that if it were true that they had made any themselves, that put a different face on things. He was new to it, knew no more than what he had been informed, that they had merely bought a few hundred tons from Carnegie, made none themselves, owed us nothing, but would pay $25,000 to dispose of the case.

Attempts to get in touch with the heads of the Biggs concern failed. No one seemed to know anything of the matter or to have any authority. As for the strange facts and events that later transpired, no one I met, of Biggs or anyone else, ever dreamed of them.

These suits drag along for years. Biggs was no exception. Churchey fumed, we all tried to get somewhere with someone or anyone in Biggs. The lawyers tried to get an authoritative meeting. Everything failed.

Churchey spent his time mostly on the Continent of Mu work, discussing with me many aspects of it, the disclosures of the Troano Manuscript and the Codex Cortesianus, the many resemblances between Egyptian and Yucatan civilizations and religions, and the growing belief on his part that the Mayans peopled the world in South America, Egypt, Greece, Persia, India, and were closely related to the great Maori race, of Oceania, of whom Churchey knew a great deal and had known many intimately. He regarded them as survivors of the sinking of Mu, or an offshoot dwelling as an early colonization upon some lands outside the main continent, though he rarely conceded that any Pacific islands could be anything but ancient mountain peaks of Mu.

I was and am deeply interested in Mu, and have always been aware of the resemblances of ancient civilizations, of the intimate relation of its main languages to one another, known since Jones and Max Muller and others showed the thread of Sanskrit and Greek and Latin and established the Indo Germanic genus, and made a new basis of modern philology. I never made any personal researches into the question, drew my knowledge of it from those I met, Le Plongeon and Churchward, and from books on allied matters, as well as from years of contemplation of thousands of facts known to me bearing upon the subject of the coordination of civilizations.

But I never spent much time on it, nor accounted it a superior interest of my life, being more devoted to physics, cosmology, philosophy and the problem of matter, motion, mind and man. I found no definite evidences deciding me as to Mu, and regarded it as an interesting theory not yet proved. Later I had more reason to consider the probabilities of Mu, when Churchey consulted me about the form of publication of his work upon it, as will appear.

Meanwhile I was busy with the commercial exploitation of Churchward steel. Wiser than before, I insisted upon an Agreement in writing giving me definitely a specified share in all verdicts and settlements. Also a Contract appointing me sole Sales Director for America, to make all licenses to manufacture and sell the steel. In this Contract I agreed to turn over to the Churchward Company the amount of royalties they had been asking per ton on the steel, my compensation to be simply what royalty above that figure I could secure by making the steel a more attractive and marketable proposition; I would take none of the Churchward share. I relied on reducing the cost or showing reason for paying adequately for this valable steel. I counted on my salesmanship to secure orders myself from users of alloy steels, at such prices that a mill would gladly pay such percentage as would give the Churchward Company its dues, and myself a good profit.

    I immediately got in touch with mills which had been making this steel secretly or otherwise. The United Alloy Steel Corporation of Canton, Ohio, made a license contract with me, under which we cooperated to deliver a considerable quantity of Churchward steel.

    United Alloy was a $40,000,000 company, very well known. Years back, when Henry Ford was young and struggling, he tried to get the big mills to make him special steels he needed for his new automobiles. No one would bother with him, he could take what they made and sold or leave it. Except Harry R. Jones, President of United Alloy, who went out of his way to provide Ford with any steels he ordered.

When Ford became big, Steel salesmen of the larger mills, and their executives, came to him and offered him cut rates to get his trade. Ford's answer was Ford-like:

> Those days when I was too small for you to bother with, Harry Jones made me what I wanted. My business goes to him up to his mill's capacity. Price wouldn't move me. He will charge me the least he can and make a fair profit.

It had been reported to me by several that Harry Jones was aloof, reserved and difficult. Hard to handle. I found that when cards were placed down on the table face up, Harry Jones was easy to work with, affable and most likable.

I then went after other mills. Through **excellent introductions,** I met the President of one of the largest mills outside of what were called the Big Three. I shall here call it the Formost Steel Company, for I shall quote statements made which, while ethical to disclose at this late date and time, I do not wish to pin on anyone who may not today care to father **them** on account of some changed relations with the Inside Steel and High Finance combination.

Through certain Syracuse connections I became intimate with a director of another great independent mill, which I shall call **Alembic S**teel Corporation for a like reason, though it seems almost needless when nothing is alleged against any of these concerns or people.

Both these two large steel mills, through conferences of their presidents with me, entered into oral agreements with me as follows:

They were to cease infringing the patents, recognize validity, as Carnegie had done. I would license them to make the steel, at royalties fixed per ton.

Written contracts were to be drawn and signed in due course. One of these mills contracted to make at least so much of the steel as would have made the Churchward Company and myself $60,000 a year in royalties from them.

These contracts were never completed. The president of one mill told me frankly, "I had word from New York that Steel must always stand with Steel, and they expect me to keep off recognizing your patents and taking license under them, until your suits against Biggs and others are withdrawn, decided or settled. Do you get me?"

"But look here, Mac, you are an independent concern," I protested. "You are a competitor of the U.S. Steel Corporation and of the Big Three. How do you happen to take orders from New York, from Interests back of the Big Three and do as they tell you? Judge Gary insists that there is no Trust, no Monopoly in Steel. That no one in Steel controls all Steel."

"Young man," the president replied, "You listen to me. They want us to be independent. They don't want the odium of Monopoly and prosecutions for restraint of trade. We are independents, free as the air, and rivals of the Big Three. Yes we are! As free as the air in a Westinghouse air-brake cylinder. If I happen to do just one thing New York doesn't like, a total stranger to me comes in here politely, with introductions, and says quietly, "One of our clients wanted to find out just what you are doing in Eastern Ohio. There is some complaint of price-cutting there or influencing a certain customer away or some mix-up. We wondered if you knew all about it, or cared to look into it. We want to prevent friction in Steel, and if we know what your intentions are there, we can adjust ourselves to that."

"And this means?" I inquired, much intrigued.

"It means, Griffith, that unless I speedily stop whatever is jarring someone in your New York, in my dealings in Eastern Ohio, I'll find my biggest customer in Illinois or Kentucky or Kamschatka taken away mysteriously, and some other customers I love. My mill will make a nice red figure for my stockholders that year. Perhaps some of my stockholders who have loans out may be put under pressure or influences used with some others, and I may find I have a new Board of Directors who elect a new president, if I don't own control myself. Nobody can pin a thing on anyone. No one knows about it, everyone denies blandly ever warning me on Eastern Ohio."

I confirmed this statement of Steel internal machinery in other quarters most authoritative. It was the outcome of Judge Gary's famous and beautiful dictum way back, that "there were to be no agreements, no combinations, no unlawful price-fixing. Just tell one another nicely what you are doing, and apply the Golden Rule."

The hand of the power that moves in Steel, is a grip of steel.

The Golden Rule in Steel is the Rule of Steel by Gold.

In the case of the other great mill, Alembic Steel, I went to see the Director of the Company who had contacted me with them. He was panicky. "I should never in the world have gotten into this. I must not speak. Forgive me, but you don't know the Inside of Steel. I should have considered....there were patent suits, hostilities. I may stand to lose my shirt. I am under heavy fire now. Do please pardon me, I mustn't mix in this thing further. Your deal with Alembic is of course suspended until your suits are terminated satisfactorily."

They could not cow or intimidate or soft-soap Harry R. Jones. United Alloy made our steel, until the end. What was attempted, what was done in that Corporation, I cannot even today say. I am perforce silent, unless some one else speaks. And at this late day none will.

I didn't mind too much, swimming against this undercurrent. I was making headway, making N C V steel and selling it. Tout viennent a qui sait attendre..... and hustle. I was bending every effort to reach some settlement with Biggs and other infringers. When peace was achieved, then the business would begin to flood in. All wars come to an end sometime.

Suddenly the Biggs case came to a hearing, on a motion by the Biggs attorneys setting up a strange defense, brand new to us, which in no way displeased me. At most it could only, I felt, delay us for years in getting justice.

IX.

I WIN COLONEL CHURCHWARD

A MILLION DOLLARS

THIS DEFENSE OF THE GREAT BIGGS MILL against our suit was a flash of lightning. Unanticipated by any of us. In appraising the gross and utterly horrible injustice done to Colonel Churchward by the Courts of the land, eventually, this defense will be remarked and borne in mind by everyone reading this work. This defense gave the lie direct to the final thrusts of the spear and sword into the Colonel at the end. For, without going into details of the smashing of the Colonel by the Steel Juggernaut at this place, out of its due chronological order, I have already indicated that he was given a coup de grace at last.

This defense, made by Biggs Mill, was that this Churchward patent steel was so valuable and so necessary,

<u>so uniquely superior, that when the U.S. Government gave the Biggs Mill orders for armor plates for our warships and other steel articles, which were to be of such and such quality and strength, withstand certain ballistic and other tests, there was only one steel that would satisfy the Governmental requirements and specifications, namely this Churchward steel, and so they just had to infringe the patents; they couldn't fill the orders if they didn't !!!!!</u>

This was no childish defense. It was based on Federal Law that this Government could use any patent it found necessary for its war or navy purposes, and the patentee could go to the Court of Claims for compensation, but he couldn't get out an injunction against the Government, or sue them for infringement damages.

Now, said Biggs Mill, if the Government can take a patent for its use, a Government Contractor ordered by Government to supply them with some goods, can take the patent, use it, and you can't sue him. You can only go to the Court of Claims, and ask compensation from Uncle Sam for his using your patented invention, and take what you are allowed.

So, Colonel Churchward, you invented the only steel that would do what this Government demanded a steel to do, and we had the right to use it for the Navy armor plate and other goods. Go to the Court of Claims for pay, from the Government. We get off scot-free.

Biggs Mill was not the first infringer of a patent to offer that shrewd defense. Already someone else had suggested the same alibi, and the case was up to the Supreme Court waiting its decision.... was that good law or not?

The eminent Charles Neave, Counsel for Biggs, put this up to Federal Judge Oliver Dickinson in Philadelphia, and made a brilliant argument showing that Churchward steel was the only steel they could use, so it was really done for and in behalf of the Government. Our Counsel made equally able rejoinders, and punched holes in it cleverly, but as the point was before the Supreme Court, there was no alternative for Judge Dickinson except to grant motion to postpone hearing on our case until the Supreme Court told us what was the law on it.

From my contacts with the Vice President of Biggs, with Alva Dinkey, with Ray Bolling and others in Steel, I had gotten into my head in some quasi-clairvoyant way, that the Biggs Mill had sold about 5000 tons of this steel to the Government, and that only a tenth of this had come to them from Carnegie, the rest being made by them.

After I conveyed this to our Counsel, I also had the privilege of discussing this with a Steel man, introduced to me by Churchey, who had given me many facts he would not venture to others, even the Colonel, fearing he might be quoted. He never was by me. He told me flatly the tonnage sold Biggs by Carnegie was 500 tons, and Biggs had made about ten times that, say 5000 tons in all, or possibly 5500 tons.

What I was doing to advance N C V steel, and my offers to other infringers of amnesty for fair settlement and a new contract of sale, became bruited around, and our Counsel and I were invited to meet Neave for Biggs, to see if we could agree on a compromise. Neave the erudite, **expert, and keenly honorable,** xxxxxxx **was** one of the most able patent attorneys ever practicing in America. His quietly quick grasp of a point and his wide knowledge of law, reminded me of the old dean of that bar George Harding, who had fought cases **together** with Abraham Lincoln, and was still hearty at eighty five, when I met him in my boyhood days, and in kindly sympathy with my youthful ambitions, he gave me much insight into patent principles.

Neave and I were fairly agreed on a settlement of our case against Biggs for four hundred thousand dollars. He was handicapped by Churchey's previous ill-advised offer to settle for $25,000. Neave saw that this had been due to misinformation given Churchey, and had been withdrawn, but the Biggs people clung to it. It stuck in their craw.

Here was an ironical contrast. When Carnegie Company had hurled its worst at me, proved we hadn't a case, and offered $25,000, I smashed their arguments and got in actual money $275,000. Which Churchey had complained was giving it away to them.

But when, after I had quit his steel in disgust, the Biggs people flashed the same **brand of** alibis on Churchey to show he had no case, what did he do? I asked him good-humoredly but straight from the shoulder, where was that bold warrior talk he'd favored? Did he smash their arguments and get any $275,000? No, he didn't pick up any valuable Austrian vases, fling them in fragments on the floor and demand like Napoleon, "Take my terms or I'll smash you as I've just done with this vase ", the way he told my brother Ed he'd have done, after I won him $275,000. He lay down and offered to take $25,000. I couldn't help reminding him of all this, and poking fun at him. When I got back in his steel again, I brought the Biggs settlement up to $400,000 despite his unfortunate muddling of it, and if Neave's clients had followed his wishes, I'd have had this goodly sum. As they still thought of that meagre $25,000, I told Neave I'd meet them all as I had Alva Dinkey and agree with them on a settlement in a day.

To our surprise, word came from Neave that Biggs Mill wouldn't settle, they would fight the case. Neave didn't like it. He told me frankly, "I do not wish to go to trial on this case, I wish to dispose of it." He tried his people again, but to no avail.

The legal battle was on in earnest. The Supreme Court had decided against the contention that anybody who wanted to sell goods to the Government could steal any patent he wished to. The Government could use a patent and refer the patentee to the Court of Claims, but a Contractor couldn't; he had no such right. Good law; no one ever thought it was right, it was just clever corporation lawyers' attempt to interpret.

So as the Biggs Mill could no longer use the defense that Churchward steel was so good that they just had to use it, nothing else would do the work the Government demanded, they switched to just the contrary viewpoint. Word came to me of a strange alignment of all Steel against us. Besides the usual defense, the conventional defense, that the patent isn't valid because there was a lot like it or near it before the inventor made it (which is true of almost every great or small invention in industry....the Patent Office issues all patents for "Improvements in" bottles or barrels or matches or medicines or steels or brushes) Steel was now out to show that Churchward steel wasn't any good. It had been thought good, yes, but Steel had changed its mind, and just <u>two weeks</u> after paying us $275,000 for an exclusive license for war materials, the Big Three of Steel had decided to abandon its use.

Experts would be hired to prove the steel wasn't a good steel at all. Men would be brought from big mills to swear it had been "abandoned" by them, dropped discredited. This after many years' sales of it to the Government, its withstanding all the highest Government tests of tensile strength, and ballistic tests of the Navy Department, and being used to protect our sailors and marines on our principal warships during the World War. The Navy in tests had shot heavy projectiles at Churchward steel armor plates with powerful cannon, and Churchward steel had withstood their impact and bounced them back or glanced them off. How could this be?

How could Biggs Mill first make the defense that the steel was the best steel, the only steel that would do the work and fulfill the requirements of the U.S.Government, and when that plea failed, turn about and plead that they had a right to use it because it was so poor it wasn't any good?

Do the Courts allow such absurd and contradictory defenses? They do. Biggs Mill gravely made both those defenses, first one and then the other. And Steel experts would unquestionably be willing to testify with solemn faces to either defense selected.

I went at once to Alva Dinkey. He had relinquished his high post as President of the vast Carnegie Steel Company, to take that of President of Midvale Steel which, while then a $100,000,000 corporation, was not so great as Carnegie. Alva Dinkey confided to me his reason. I am free to tell it here. Interests in Wall Street had asked him to do this, as Morgan wished Midvale to organize for furnishing war materials to the Allies, and needed Alva Dinkey there. Midvale did what was wanted and afterward supplied immense quantities of it to the U.S. Government too. The same explanation of Dinkey's change had been supplied me by ex-Patent Commissioner Seymour and his brother Fred of Seymour, Seymour & Harmon, formerly Dill Seymour & Kellogg, the law firm which had made the famous settlement between Carnegie and Frick that finally brought forth the United States Steel Corporation. Seymour & Seymour were keeping close watch on Morgan's handling of British interests, and incidentally got themselves into green and yellow limelight by so doing.

I put it up to Alva Dinkey to "show me" how this great N C V steel was no good. To explain why he had bought it up exclusively for war materials for $275,000, and in two weeks "abandoned" it as no good. "If it was no good, why didn't you show that in Court and kill our case? Why pay $275,000 for it if it was worthless? What happened in those two weeks to make it no good? How could it be the only steel that would do the work, and yet so poor it was abandoned by the big companies? How could you get it past the ballistic and tensile strength tests of the Navy Department? How get them to pay you $20,000,000 for it, if it was no good? What's the set-up?"

Dinkey smoothed it over a bit. He doubted if they would really make that defense prominently. It was perhaps just patent attorney zeal. N C V was a fine steel, he didn't have to tell me that. Carnegie knew it, he knew it, I knew it, and we all knew it. It was true they had managed to "heat-treat" the old style cheaper steels to get them past the Government tests, and were no longer using the costly N C V except for special cases where it was especially needed, like conning towers and protective deck-plate.

Naturally I protested vigorously against such an improper attack on our steel. "Why, Dinkey, you know this steel is the finest in the world for armor plate. Your old steels may have been bolstered up to get by, but how does that alter the fact that N C V is the same stout steel it always was? "

Dinkey was disturbed but still felt it wouldn't amount to anything. He would see them, and tell them not to press such a point. "They can't get away with it. Why try it? " he remarked.

Then he volunteered what seemed a solution of the matter. "Griffith, this whole fight ought to be killed. I will get hold of President Harkins (this name I use instead of the true one, for reasons given before) and arrange a meeting between you two....I'll be there if he likes... and you both can get rid of this mess I'm sure. "

This suited me to a tee. President Harkins of Biggs Mill was a keen square steel man of unusual ability. I could talk to such a man, and win him to a deal. "I'll promise you I'll give him my shirt if need be to reach a compromise. But why not Briggs? Briggs is the backbone of Biggs Mill and its founder. I wish you could find out why Briggs is said to be down on Colonel Churchward."

Dinkey smiled. "Yes, my relations with Briggs are close, but when I tell you I've never been in any of his companies, you may draw your own inferences."

I do not wish anyone to form the conclusion that because I use the names Biggs, Harkins and Briggs in this connection, and previously Formost Steel and Alembic Steel, that I do so because there was anything done by any of these concerns or persons, which was wrongful and censurable. I neither defend nor assault what is done in business and in law. Things that are done by corporations are often done in part by this one who knows little of the whole affair, that one who does what a superior orders on the strength of what someone else inaccurately judged, or some lawyer who was out to beat the other side. Invariably, there is no one there to present the opposite side, and its equities. A business concern's rivals and enemies are just foes who must be wrong and must be beaten by all lawful means.

  Because I do not wish anyone to form a wrong opinion of "Biggs" or "Harkins", Formost or Alembic Steel, when their side isn't presented by them here, I use these names, although I have made it clear that I do not allege anyone of them did anything improper. In any place or time when these concerns or people can state their viewpoint, and lambaste old Churchey and his steel in return, I should be very glad to mention names fully; and still will not be accusing them of wrong.

  I hold a different letter of marque against the _system_ of Business, the _system_ of High Finance, the _system_ of Inside Steel, the _system_ of Law and Courts, by which so many wrongs are done, including distinct wrong to Churchward and Churchward steel. Each decade [generation or century] these things may and do improve, and stout words to help that along are the duty of all who know, and know what and why.

  Alva Dinkey, President of Midvale Steel, for-

merly President of Carnegie when we made out $275,000
settlement, phoned me at my home at Stamford that President Harkins of Biggs Mill agreed to meet me to dispose
of the case, and Harkins would communicate with me naming
a date. I was elated. I knew I could show this right-thinking, clear-seeing man why we ought to do so. I promised the Churchward associates that I would win out on
it, or eat my hat. "In the manner of Chesterton's hero"
Churchey jibed, "who made a hat out of a cabbage before
eating it to pay his wager."

This meeting was never arranged. Why I do not
know to this day. I phoned Harkins. He was out but his
secretary knew of it, assured me that meeting would be set,
and that they would write me the date. Still not hearing,
I saw Dinkey, but all he could tell me was that it was off,
he did not know why and could not surmise.

The case was set for trial. The honest frank
Lawyer Neave, learning from his clients that they had made
most of the steel buying only part from Carnegie, phoned
us to tell us what he knew, before trial. That was Neave
all through; a "good sport and a good scout" in the vernacular. The amounts were just what I had previously doped
out: about 5000 tons in all, one-tenth of it from Carnegie,
nine-tenths Biggs Mill's own manufacture and own infringement, about $4,000,000 worth.

Just before we left for Philadelphia, where the
case was to be heard, a species of bombshell burst. Not a

shrapnel shell by any means, but an illuminating shell that threw streams and flares of light around. We received a cordial and friendly letter from the Patent Lawyer of the Carnegie Company, D.A. Usina, asking us to give Carnegie a license to manufacture Churchward steel for commercial purposes. He said that since we sold Carnegie the exclusive right for this steel for war materials, the commercial demand and use of it was increasing, and they had demands to supply it. Would we like to give them a license to make it for commercial purposes?

Would we? As the Italian said, "Would swimma da duck?" We certainly would. But what a parcel of dynamite this was ! Here all Steel, the experts and makers of Steel, were going to swear our steel was "abandoned" by them as no good, and here was Usina the very lawyer who was to appear in Court representing Carnegie, begging us for a further license to make it more extensively !

I went over to see Usina. He "felt certain because of our peaceful and friendly relations and the amount of this steel we could make and the royalties we'd pay you, that you would be agreeable." He would write making an appointment with President Williams of Carnegie, Dinkey's successor, who wished to meet me.

Then came the trial. A problem came up. Should we put Colonel Churchward on the stand? He was inventor of the steel, also president of his company. He could not prove infringement by Biggs, but he could tell of his experiences in their mill and others. Unfortunately old Churchey's memory was treacherous and undependable. On being examined by his Counsel in advance, he had his facts correctly, but in terribly mixed sequence. Things which he one moment said happened first and other things after, he reversed later, and wouldn't see the difference. He showed the effects of the years and the strain he had been under.

He was so antagonized by the two-faced defense, which first had delayed his case a long time by claiming it was the only steel that would do the work, and then came forward to claim that per contra it was worthless; that he insisted upon reprisals by testifying, and demanding subpoenaing of witnesses to prove, that in one mill where he was experimenting, in his early making of the steel, a large crane had dumped tons of white-hot steel on a spot he had just left on a providential hint from On High. This to Churchey was the keynote of the whole case, and the most important issue. The fight was to be made on that. It was one fact that no one could approve or palliate. When the Court learned what Steel had attempted to do to him, to steal his invention and kill him because "dead men tell no tales", there would no longer be any mercy shown any steel mill infringer, no matter whether it had anything to do with that episode or not.

The lawyers were disturbed. Churchey refused to appear on the stand unless he were allowed to tell this, and a whole lot of other things he had learned from his underground sources in Steel, which would show up the whole of the Industry as it should be. The fact that these matters might be hearsay or irrelevant, meant nothing at all to the Colonel. He was a veteran fighter in wars and riots, in business scraps, and no one could tell him how he should or shouldn't fight. Give 'em no quarter! He'd run the campaign that way or he wouldn't appear.

In addition, there had been two incidents which not only had bearing on the question of using him as a witness, but also have momentous weight in connection with what I shall have to tell about his Lost Continent of Mu. So much, that I give them here in full.

On his visits to me at Stamford, and mine to his estate at Lakeville, I had found many evidences of his failing memory. Of these, two stand out. He showed me a fine St. Lawrence River skiff, some twenty feet long, which he used for fishing and rowing about in the Lake. "This skiff was specially designed and built for me by the Blank works up North there. Major Blank himself did it. He put his best thoughts and timbers into it, and built it according to my directions. He made it so a 250 lb. man could stand on the gunwale and it won't tip over." And so on, with meticulous detail.

I hadn't the heart to tell my old friend there was one item he had omitted. He had clean forgotten that some years ago I had myself made him a present of this skiff, which I had selected from stock in New York, and still had on the various marks identifying it.

The old chap may have confused this more recently acquired boat with some other he had owned in the

139

deep past. Forty years before he had fished the St. Lawrence. Later, in my boyhood, we had both fished there for weeks at a time, and caught each trip hundreds of bass, scores of large pickerel, and our share of the monster muskallonge that were taken by the initiated.

On another visit, he had shown myself and others an "old Mayan knife" a dagger, made 3000 years back by colonists of Mu residing in India or Burma, who had come there either before or as a sequence of its blow-up. Churchey described how this knife came into his possession, and showed us the design evidencing its age,(as though any designs of Burmese art weren't copied for centuries, and even today !). It bore no impress of thirty centuries or of any great age. It was of usual Hindu workmanship. On one part of the blade, blurred almost off, I deciphered a tiny printed "Sheffield, Eng." Aside, I showed him this.

He said he had picked the knife up in India for a few rupees half a century ago, but thought it was very old, from its pattern of decoration. In one of his books he mentions this knife, and I believe states that the blade had probably been replaced, and only the **haft was** 3000 years old. It was no more 3000 than you or I are. Churchey hugged his delusions. He couldn't let them go, even when he knew inwardly they were punctured. This is the clue to certain features in his Mu books to which I shall refer in due course. He was honestly self-fooled at times.

The lawyers had a final talk with Churchey, and he decided not to appear as a witness. There was little he could have testified to, that wasn't fully admitted, except his experiences with the infringers, and the lawyers disliked muckraking and vituperation, unproved assertions. What good were true facts mixed with wrong dates? He had recently gone through a siege of pneumonia, almost fatal, which had left him enfeebled. This illness, it was thought, may have weakened his memory, for I could tell that the old soldier was trying to do his duty, to remember accurately all he undertook to relate.

Before leaving I had an interview with a man high in Steel. He knew Judge Dickinson, who was to hear the case. "You have there a very fine judge. No power on earth could reach him and move him or try to. He is apt to form an early impression of a case and then is hard to change. He has been told in a clever way, that your Churchward is an upstart, his company a paper company and his patents paper patents. That's all."

When we got to Court, we found an array of lawyers for Biggs Mill, Carnegie, Midvale and United States Steel Counsel. It was whispered we were fighting $10,000-a-day of lawyers. Gallant Neave conceded the infringement, and relieved us of proving it. His defenses would be the conventional "it was all known before", "we made it first", "not enough to be an invention", and then the chief defense: he brought witnesses, not only experts but also men employed in Biggs and other conpanies, to say that they had all "abandoned" its use, as no good. If it was no good, it wasn't a useful invention. If not useful, then no patent on it was valid.

All this before the same Judge Oliver Dickinson, in the same court-room, where only a short time before, the same lawyer had pleaded for the same defendant, in this same case, that they had been obliged to infringe our patent and use our steel because it was the only steel that would fulfill the Government requirements.

Plato said: "Great is the power of words. Words can make this way, can make that way."

Great is the power of Law. Law can make this way, can make that way.

Great is the power of Steel. Steel can make this way, can make that way.

Churchward steel is the finest steel in the world when we show why we had to use it, and couldn't employ any other. It alone withstands the ballistic and other tests.

But.....when that defense blows up, and a new defense is needed, then Churchward steel becomes a pauper steel, worthless, an outcast, with every hand of Inside Steel turned against it, with the Courts begged to cancel its patents because it is so bad it doesn't deserve to have a patent.

Outside the Court room, the proud ships of the American Navy sailed the Atlantic, protected by Churchward steel against any projectiles that could be hurled against their N C V-armored sides; projectiles that could pierce any other armor previously made.

In the Court room, witnesses from the large companies repeated that they had "been told by their superiors" to "abandon" Churchward steel, as it wasn't good. It used to be their white-haired boy, their pride and joy, but no more. It was "out".

While they spoke, there sat Dinkey, the President of Carnegie, who had paid me $275,000 for exclusive license to make Churchward steel for the Government, two weeks before the order to "abandon it" and recognized the validity of the patents for it. Dinkey, who had seen it tested. Dinkey, who had sold $20,000,000 of it to Uncle Sam. Dinkey, who told me it was all nonsense to make such a defense...."they can't get away with it; so why try it? I'll speak to them about it. "

There stood Neave, who had told me, "Frankly, I don't want to try this case, " and had been willing to okay a payment of $400,000 to us for use of this socalled "worthless " steel, years after its "abandonment" as no good. Neave, who had, despite that "abandonment", pronounced the steel the only one which would do the work.

And at a table sat smiling, jolly Usina, Lawyer for the Carnegie Company, listening to this defense, who only a few days before, in his own office, had written us for a license to make it for commercial needs on account of its increasing demand, had talked with me about that, had written to President Williams of Carnegie to make the appointment he desired with me, to arrange for that license.

I stared around at all these lawyers and men, who knew the worth of Churchward steel, and who sat there while these underlings, sent to say certain things, said them. And I thought of the tune played by the band at Cornwallis' Surrender at Yorktown, "The World Turned Upside Down".

Slowly, suavely, discreetly, our lawyers brought out other facts from these witnesses. They only knew what they had been told to do and say. None of the heads of the concerns who had ordered the "abandonment" testified. It wasn't clear who had ordered the old steels bolstered up with heat treatments, and used instead.

Judge Dickinson, who had been regarding me under bushy lashes, with hawk eyes, began to listen intently. "Did you tell the Government you had found this steel you had sold them no good? " "Did you pay back the money you received for that bad steel?" "Did you replace it with good steel?" Had they stripped it off and told Uncle Sam it imperilled our defenses, our Navy, and put on new plates?

No, but Counsel drew out that wherever, as in conning towers and protective deck plates and other especially vulnerable points, extra protection was needed, they had continued to furnish the Churchward steel. Also to the Italian and other foreign Governments, who refused to take the old steel instead. How could this be so, if the Churchward steel were no good? No one could answer.

Judge Dickinson was intrigued. He wanted to know how they induced the Government to let them "abandon" this steel and substitute the old steel bolstered up. It crept out that the Government didn't know that. The Steel Companies' contracts were drawn to provide for a steel that would stand such and such tests. There was some discretion as to alloys employed.

Someone in Steel had gotten Uncle Sam to raise the price from $400 a ton to $800, because they were giving him a steel that had costly alloys in it. Then when they went back to the old steel, was it likely they would ask him to reduce the price back to the old $400 a ton? If they saved costly alloys, they weren't philanthropists.

The Judge I fear didn't quite like it. Still less when it appeared that first the Carnegie bought up the exclusive rights for Government materials, so no one else could ever sell Churchward steel to the Government, and then just two weeks after that had "abandoned" its use, and its action had been followed or joined by other steel companies selling the Government steels.

Perhaps the Judge wondered why his Court wasn't honored with the presence and testimony of the heads of all the Steel companies who had so ordered, to tell him why;

Then they put on some experts to back them up. One of them, dean of experts, whom I shall call Harris, to avoid criticising a deceased expert, said he did not approve of N C V steel. It used to rate high, but not now. We had been informed that the War Department had tested this steel in the War, and that Harris knew of it. But he didn't. A small lot had gotten some vanadium in it, but it didn't amount to anything.

Our lawyers then asked me to take the stand, which I did, staying there for two days. I told all I knew about the steel. Its tests, the gradually growing commercial use of it. The high cost, which limited its use ordinarily. I showed it was used for roller-bearings and for gears and other purposes. I described my experience with it, and my dealings with Alva Dinkey and Linthicum and others.

As the various lawyers cross-examined, I made it a point to concede every fact as asked, and to offer everything they wanted, whether it helped their side or mine. I laid cards down on the table; here are the facts, let the Court form its own conclusions, I am just a witness.

I had been informed that Dinkey had his orders to testify that he had ordered the "abandonment" of the steel. It was a hard position for him. Not only his high post in Steel was at stake, he must do as he was told by High Finance and High Authority in Steel; but his loyalty to the rule that "Steel must stand by Steel ".

I knew he had received a subpoena in the case, and was to follow me on the stand, to contradict my testimony. I was not surprised when Lawyers, after bringing out my relations with Dinkey, asked me very shrewdly, if I "admitted Dinkey was an eminent and careful business man, who knew what he was **about**".

Much amused at this, knowing its reason, I answered **straight** from the shoulder, " Yes, and also a man of unquestioned honesty and integrity." The lawyers could hardly believe their ears. Why, this gave Dinkey's evidence the cachet of my own guarantee; I couldn't challenge anything he said, after that. "Then if he testifies differently from you in this matter, you concede ...." I replied, "I will wait and listen respectfully to what Alva Dinkey testifies to here."

Alva Dinkey had stepped out of the room for a while and was not present when I said this. Upon being informed of it, and the wide-open road I left him, he withdrew from the case and refused to testify. He told me afterward that he had "declined flatly to help any such defense, and they could all go to hell before he would be any party to it."

Dinkey's lawyer, Charles C. Linthicum, who had negotiated the $275,000 settlement with me first and then second in company with Dinkey, was dead. Somehow the drift of the case seemed to leave an implication against Linthicum. Had he mismanaged this point or concealed that from me? Did we feel any blame attached to him? No open question came up so I could answer, No, indeed. It was just there, in the atmosphere of the suit. I did not intend to have any reflection rest on this fine lawyer. So when his name came up again, I asked permission to stop for a few moments in my testimony out of respect to the memory of Linthicum, "whose name I cannot speak here in this Court without pausing just briefly in tribute to his genial spirit and many glorious qualities".

Something made me look at Judge Dickinson after I finished. There were tears in his eyes, and in those of many of the lawyers. That night I learned that Linthicum had been the dearest personal friend of Judge Dickinson, who often consulted him on points of patent law in cases.

This innocent incident, actuated by fair play

to a dead man of noble character, was used as part of the silly story spread throughout Steel, that I had hypnotised Judge Dickinson.

I finished my recital by telling of the Carnegie Company, which had "abandoned" our steel as no good, applying to me for a license to make it for commercial trade. Lawyer Usina jumped up in excitement, fathered it and his letter, and sought to explain.

This was certainly some T.N.T. Neave looked at Usina in astonishment. Other lawyers in the room did likewise. Judge Dickinson could hardly credit what he was hearing. He had listened to so much that was unusual.

Some of the great Steel Companies had sold Uncle Sam $20,000,000 worth of Churchward steel, getting a double price for it, putting it through remarkable tests to meet Government specifications. Hadn't told Churchward nor paid him royalties, though they had been in touch with him, had been shown his steel and how to make it. They had made it for years. Carnegie had paid us $275,000 for the war-rights. At times, Carnegie made some and gave part to others to sell to the Navy.

Right in his Court, lawyers for Biggs had told Judge Dickinson it was so good they just had to use it. It was on our ships during the War. Projectiles couldn't pierce it.

Then two weeks after Carnegie had bought it up, from me, and no one else could supply it, they dropped it, and substituted the old steel, but hadn't told Uncle Sam they were changing back from Churchward steel to the other, nor that they had sold him for $20,000,000 steel that was "no good" or "abandoned".

They had sent under men here to say it was no good, but the heads who had so decided hadn't come, not one of them. And the witnesses admitted that for especially vulnerable points they still supplied the Churchward steel.

And while they were coming to his Court to tell him how poor our steel was, and he ought to kill our patents because our steel was so useless, Carnegie through its own Patent Lawyer had begged us to let them have the right to make more of it.

Judge Dickinson was visibly annoyed. He let them all know he didn't take any stock in their defense. He warned them right out in Court that he didn't feel they had made out a case.

As he said this, pacing up and down as was his wont, he stood with his hands on my shoulders as I sat in the witness chair. Everyone in Court stared at the almost paternal way in which this highly esteemed and venerated Judge did this, as he told them, in the vernacular, "where they got off".

This was also quoted widely in Steel in furtherance of the claim that this Griffith had "hypnotized Judge Dickinson".

144

Three weeks later, Judge Dickinson handed down a decision sustaining the Churchward patents, finding infringement, issuing a permanent injunction against them, and ordering an accounting and payment to us of all their immense profits made from the manufacture and sale of Churchward steel.

Conservatively estimated, this was a verdict for over One Million dollars.

When I had quit Churchward steel, Churchey had been ready to settle with Biggs mill for $25,000. Upon my re-entry into it, the case had changed till it culminated in this decision for a million dollars.

Since the Judge had decided the case practically standing back of me in the witness chair, before any arguments of Counsel on the various sides, Steel was so startled at this that no one could shake it from the conviction gradually formed by a whispering campaign, that I had hypnotised the Judge.

While all in the world I had done, had been to lay my cards down face up, in Court, as I had with Steel, and stand on the facts, with no care for the outcome if only those in authority to decide, had those facts before them. With Othello," this only was the magic I had used "to get old Churchey's steel sold widely, to win Linthicum and Dinkey to pay me $275,000, to get Lawyer Neave anxious to settle for $400,000, to get Dinkey to quit the case by simply giving his testimony, whatever it might be, the accolade of honesty and integrity, and to get Judge Dickinson to render a rightful verdict of this large amount.

X.

THE LAW GIVETH AND THE LAW TAKETH AWAY

ONE MILLION DOLLARS ! It is an immense sum to anyone not a multi-millionaire. Almost none at all of the two billion to two billion and a half of all the peoples of earth ever own a million dollars. Just a few moneyed rulers of men.

This time Churchey met wealth with dignity. He shed honest tears of gratitude over my hands as he held them, and assured me I shouldn't be chiseled out of my own share this time.....and it was a goodly amount.

All we both ever needed forever. If....IF.. we had ever collected any of it.

Here, however, is where Steel began to show us things. And so did Law. Naturally the Biggs Mill lawyers lodged an appeal. And these cases take time.

I did not let any grass grow under my feet. I sallied forth to button up every steel corporation and get every mill turning out Churchward steel for the various industries that could use it.

Frames of cars. Gears. Roller-bearings. Axles and shafts. Railway materials. Bridge elements. Housings and framework of machines, for greater strength with lighter weight. Wherever steel was used that called, not for hardness as in cutting tools, but toughness as as in stress-carrying metal. My ambitions for N C V knew no limits other than those of practicability. Cost must be brushed aside if strength and durability were desired, though I soon met the cost issue with pike and battle-ax.

But everywhere I went, even though I made headway, I found that Steel was still not free. There was a current against which we must swim, and in most cases could by no means whatever breast. So long as the case was on Appeal, Steel was still expected by Steel to await the final verdict.

And good friends began to assure me that this Appeal was going to be decided against us. How could anyone know that? Well may one ask. In our system of justice, no one can. The case must be heard, the judges must determine it. Till then, no one knows or can know.

But the undercurrent of Steel told me it knew or thought it knew. The President of Formost Steel (as I have called it) said to me, "Don't be a sap, Griffith. It's in the bag. No, I know no one can bribe a Federal Judge. Anyone trying would get in Dutch quickly. Not that it hasn't been done in some isolated cases, I suppose. But who put 'em in ? Who knows 'em intimately, like I know Jim Smith and Dick Jones ? Who was a law partner when the Judge was practicing? Who plays bridge with him? Who advised him on some investments and made him money? Who stands ready to groom him for some high office.?Who hints of the Supreme Court some day? Who maybe discusses with him who ought to be favored for President ? Who is a leader of the same party the Judge has ardently adhered to all his career ? "

"Good so far", I replied, "but then what?"

"Would you like to know the inside of how it is handled? Then listen. I had a case......"

He outlined it. I knew it well. Thousands have read it in law-books and probably wondered, as I did.

"We lost in the Federal Court. Patent kicked out. We wanted to save that patent. We filed an Appeal. I retained Senator Blank. I gave him carte blanche on fees. He could name any price in reason in his bill, and Blank knew how to charge. Fees in the five figures didn't frighten him, if they were on his bill-heads, and represented ethical and proper work for big interests on which such bills were quite customary and routine."

"The Senator came back to me and instructed me what to do and what not to do. Who to retain to argue my Appeal, what to tell him to say, and have him consult the

Senator about it. How to swing the case along certain lines, He told me what I might expect the verdict to be. I wouldn't win out on all counts, I couldn't keep my own shirt and also win my opponents' shirt at the same time. But I'd have all I wanted; my own was safe. And I knew it before it went through, just as it came out."

"I see", I answered. This was clever; as expressed, it was just good prediction by Blank of the likely outcome if his wise advice as a fine expert in law were followed; but it had resulted as he said. "I see now. I always marveled at just how that verdict was reached. It patted you on the back and gave you the decision, but when I looked to see how it lambasted the other side accordingly, I found they also got a pat on the back and also got the decision. The verdict practically read, Joe Green is right and therefore his opponent Mike Brown is also right. Joe has been kayo'd by Mike, and Mike has also been kayo'd by Joe. 'The winnahs !....Joe Green, champion against everyone but Mike; and Mike Brown, champion undefeated and unbeatable.' I never could grasp it before."

"You can now, young man. Go and settle with your big Steel enemies and get going in the markets. You and I can do business; we are 'both practical men' ".

Once more we tried to settle with Biggs, even though we had the verdict. We would give them a good break in every way, and meet to discuss amount of settlement on any fair basis, the same as if we hadn't won this amount of judgment against them. But nothing came of it. All we could do was wait, and try to sell steel meanwhile.

Churchey was much disturbed and depressed by the rumors of defeat looming up for us on this Appeal. I saw much of him those days, both at my home and in New York and in Lakewood. He spent much of his time on Mu, talking Mu, thinking Mu. If we won the Appeal and got all that money, we would go to Yucatan and the South Seas, and rout out evidences of Mu and the Mayans. The same energies I had employed in working up this Steel affair, would churn up a complete solution of all questions about Mu.

If however we lost the Appeal as he feared, then he would take all his mass of data and writings, memos and notes, and work up that material into a book, which would utterly confound all his enemies who would believe his steel had been his greatest achievement, while millions read avidly his works on Mu, and acclaimed him as an explorer and archaeologist.

One day buoyed up and confident, another day despondent and pessimistic, Churchey began to widen the scope of his hostility to Steel, into a general suspicion of all big business. To him, every captain of industry and every known Wall Street leader, was a despoiler of the small man. They would all rob anyone of everything he had, if it were large enough.

"Larceny" said Churchey to me one day, "runs in grades, according to the amount of money in it. Steal a little, it's petty larceny, and you go to jail for six months. Steal a lot, and you go there for five or ten years, that's grand larceny. But if the amount is inordinately high, millions are involved, and you hire shrewd corporation lawyers and heavy respectable lawyers who are cronies of the judges and politicians, it isn't petty or grand, it's legalized larceny and you don't go to jail for a minute; you either get away with it if your lawyers and drag beat the other side, or pay back part of the money stolen if they beat you, in the Courts. The more larceny, the more of the swag goes to the lawyers who are in partnership with the thieves. On petty larceny, the lawyers get $50 to $100. On grand larceny, the lawyers get $1000 to $3000 of it. On legalized larceny, the lawyers get $50,000 to $250,000 out of it."

Besides pushing N C V steel, I also owned properties and had buildings erected on lands I held, owning likewise a couple of realty companies, and was obliged to look after these interests. I had that Winter a goodly fight on my hands. My brother having died since I sold out my insurance interest to him, left affairs of his in condition calling for my aid. The insurance company, because of the age of the surviving partner, E.E.Clapp, sought to kill the contract between them and take over the business arduously built up bu decades of struggle. My old partner Clapp being helpless against this, I was asked to take up cudgels in behalf of him and my brother's estate. After six months of negotiations, I arranged a compromise by which the insurance company bought up the goodwill of the business for some $150,000, which placed both partners on a safe basis for life, I also made it a condition of settlement that the firm's assistant manager for many years be retained at a salary of $15,000 per annum (he became one of the best-posted and popular managers in that line today.)

Churchey took this contest as another instance of how, he thought, all corporations are out to do everybody and grasp all loose change in their paths. Yet he was not at all sympathetic with the laboring producers of the world, who live under the two-fold burden of receiving as producers of wealth but a small part of the product of their labor, and of having as consumers to buy such products of labor at exorbitant market prices.

There was an instance of this at my home in Stamford when he was calling. I was building some houses on some lands at Shippan, and various builders combined to reduce the wages of carpenters from $8 a day to $6. I declined to join such a move. As I wasn't a builder, just an owner, the builders went on without me, and notified the men of the new rate. The carpenters came to me for advice.

"It's quite enough for them," Churchey declared. "In England I think they get eight shillings. I remember when men asked for eight shillings as a high rate. Had a slogan they sang: Eight hours'work; eight hours play;eight hours' sleep; eight shillings a day. It's enough. $8 is too much, Perc."

His anecdote gave me an idea. I advised the carpenters:

"Meet the bosses tonight. Don't argue or say a word, except to carry a big banner, point to it, and in-sist, **This** is our only answer: On that banner, have printed, in immense letters:

> Eight hours' work,
> Eight hours' play,
> Eight hours' sleep,
> Eight dollars a day.

They did this and won their fight. Rightly. In a few years, none would deny that.

Churchey had come to urge me to try once more to get Alva Dinkey to influence Harkins of Biggs Mill to settle our suit, before their Appeal was heard. "Dinkey is strong for you, Perc. His refusal to testify and throwing down Biggs and Morgan and Gary for you, is well-known in Steel. It has made him loom bigger than ever. Win him to engineering a compromise. He can do it. I'm afraid of your Courts over here; I hear too many stories."

Dinkey asked me to come to Pittsburg. He was most despondent when I arrived. Distraught, with his attention elsewhere. I asked him what was the trouble. "I don't know what to do, Griffith. I've been ordered to cut wages 10%. There'll be a strike. Bloodshed. I went through the Homestead strike, and I know what it means. Riot, stones, bricks attack on the plant, deaths. Business stopped. Costly to both sides. Poverty and starvation to the strikers. I can't face it. What would you do?"

The delegates are due in a half hour.

I told him the story of the carpenters, but he didn't favor that $8 wage. The country couldn't pay carpenters $8 a day and continue to exist. But he insisted that

I give him my solution of his mess. At last, seeing he meant this, though I was a mere tyro in Steel, with no experience as worker or boss in a steel mill, I replied: "Why not, instead of laying down a 10% cut and causing a strike, say this to your men:

> Boys, we are all in one boat, the Mill. Prices have fallen all around us. Last year we sold this much steel to the farmer for a bushel of wheat; this much for a bushel of corn or oats; so much steel to the hat-maker for a gross of hats; so much for a gross of gloves or shoes.
> Now, at the price of those things and the price of steel, we are asking them all to give us, for the same amount of steel, two bushels of wheat, corn and oats instead of one, two gross of hats, gloves or shoes. The same amount of steel as last year we sold them for one bushel or one gross. They won't pay. They won't buy our steel unless we....you and I and all of us....lower the price.
> What do you wish me to do? Shut down the Mill till prices improve? You boys have the big stake in this. You say the word.

Dinkey jumped up. "I'll do it, Griffith. Try it anyway. Come back in an hour and I'll tell you how it comes out."

When I returned, the great executive, big-hearted captain of men, was on top of the world. The men listened, asked him if he could keep the mill open with economies by all. How much cut in wages, temporarily, would help out? Dinkey put it up to them. They suggested 10%. He agreed to try it.

There was no strike in Midvale. There were strikes elswhere, as wages fell from the inflated level they had reached. In Canton, Ohio, I left the United Alloy plant at 3.30 P.M with President Harry Ross Jones. We drove past groups of gesticulating strikers. "Just debating politics", laughed Jones. But one hour later nearly a thousand men and women stormed the mill and as each car drove out of the yard, it was stoned and all its windows broken, and the occupants wounded.

If we had waited until 4.30 to leave, we'd have met the same attack. I, a visitor, innocent of any share in the scrap, would have met the fate of the others, though I had been the means of averting a strike in Midvale shortly before.

My sympathies are with the men on economic and social-justice grounds. But violence is absolutely indefensible. Violence is the Neanderthal atavism of those who would kill and maim equally whether right or wrong in a given dispute, who care nothing who is right, and are incapable of deciding who is right.

All one can say of it is that when a few men, by power of money and overlordship, are ruling tens of thousands in one plant, millions in Industry, they stand much the same as sovereigns of all times ruling by force or divine right, inheritance or even votes. If the Few do not govern for the best good of the Many, then right or wrong the Many will rebel and riot, employ intimidation and the sit-down strike, **all manner of violence.**

My own answer is a system of equity in Industry and Finance and Government which will render such conflicts impossible, while also avoiding the Avernian descent to Communism which the upholders of present injustice and out-of-date arrangements are doing more to cause and assist than all the propaganda of Moscow. To say more here is disproportionate and irrelevant.

After our talk over the strike, and its succesful avoidance, Dinkey discussed Churchward steel with me, and offered to try once more to get the case disposed of. "I can't see what Briggs and Harkins are thinking of. They didn't get away with that defense in Court, and they won't on appeal. There's too much dynamite in all this abandonment talk. First thing they know, demagogues will be making a muss over the thing. I sold 'em $20,000,000 of it, and I don't want anyone coming and telling me I sold my own country steel that wasn't the very best I had, better than any other they could get to protect our sailors."

"How about substituting the old steel at the extra price of the Churchward steel?"

"Oh, that was okay. We got it worked up by heat-treatments so it filled the bill. But politicians looking for trouble will make capital out of it. I don't like anything about it, Griffith, and never did."

I then guardedly mentioned that all over I heard the same story that the appeal was definitely going to go against us. Yes, he had heard that, but it was just boasting of "loose-tongued people who thought their case was strong. No one could control Federal Judges. You could tell that from your own experience with Judge Dickinson. We don't want to fix judges and wouldn't dare. What people talk of a lot, is simply this. Steel retains big lawyers, some by the year, some on occasions. Some of them may be Senators. They are strong in politics and statesmanship. They do become judges sometimes. They do know judges like brothers. They may have been partners of judges. They belong to the same party as some judges perhaps. Some of them may have helped judges get their jobs. In a big case one of these eminent lawyers goes into the case for us and advises us. We follow his advice. If he says settle, we do; if he says fight, we fight. It is possible his connections may enable him to ask some judge, or talk to him about the law of it. We don't know that, and don't want to, and we don't demand it of him. That's all there is to any of this talk about any case at all, I'm sure."

I commented then, and here now, that it was enough and perhaps too much. Knowing nothing of any such retainers in Churchey's cases, I of course have always taken the position that Federal Courts are beyond any suspicion and their decisions are simply the best judgment of the Court on the law and the facts, as they see them.

As to general practice of some eminent lawyers other than this Churchward case, in handling cases of big business, there is much that might be said on this subject. <u>I know what I know.</u>

Meanwhile I was engaged in some important work in proving the merits of Churchward steel. I found it so highly desirable in gears that, despite its cost, I got it adopted widely.

In the New Process Gear Corporation plant at Syracuse, New York, through the courtesy of Bert Gold and J.Allan Smith the President of New Process and also of

U.S.Light & Heat Company at Niagara Falls, (that rare executive who was a technician to the ground and up, an able director, and superb seller of goods) I discovered that after the gears were finished, the percentage rejected ran into 20% to 40%. A few cents' worth of steel, with all the costs of gear-making and plant-overhead, turned into a two dollar gear. Now on microscopic inspections and tests you have to throw out a fifth or two-fifths of the finished product, and look at the loss! Instead of paying 4¢ or 5¢ a pound for an alloy steel with that result, you would surely do better with your pocket-book to pay $7\frac{1}{2}$¢ for N C V steel, if you could save most of those rejections. And I proved you could.

N C V steel reduced the rejections down to about 2%. This is no propaganda, the patents have expired, anyone can make N C V steel now, and I have not the slightest interest in it financially. I simply showed that if you made gears out of common alloy steels which left even 20% bad, you were throwing money to the dogs by not using N C V and saving many thousands of dollars.

I also found by contacts with the old expert gear-cutters there, that with Churchward steel they could run their gear-cutting machines faster than with common alloy steels. This other steel was too resistant, this second one too soft and cheesy, but N C V ran smoothly through the machine. You didn't have to run it slowly for N C V. This meant that each expensive machine, each expert machinist, turned out more gears per day, thus again reducing cost.

In gears, therefore, Churchward steel changed its status from that of the costliest steel to use, prohibitively costly, to the position of the cheapest steel to use; failure to use it meant heavy loss of money.

Out in use in cars, rear-end gears which used to crack under the strains of service, stood up nobly with N C V. This could not help augmenting sales.

But one of the strange evidences of the queer undertows and under-cover workings of Steel manifested itself. While N C V was being used more and more commercially, various steel textbooks and handbooks which previously featured N C V steel, in their newer editions omitted all mention of it. For several years, since the "abandonment" of this steel for armor plate, steel literature had been censored. By whom I do not know nor could anyone, I believe, tell today.

Dinkey reported to me that Biggs Mill was "sot" on fighting, and that there was no dice on settling. And so came on the hearing of the Appeal against the verdict we had won. It was short. The Appeals Judges had read the testimony, and Judge Dickinson's decision in our favor.

Chief Justice Buffington, a kindly and worthy old jurist, refused to sit on the case. He came over to me in Court and said, "I'm going to sit on the sidelines with you instead of on the bench. My old friend Jimmie Briggs (name disguised as before) is greatly concerned in this Appeal, and I decided to keep out of it. Though, as I tell Jimmie(the jurist's eyes twinkled) he's always so wrong about everything that maybe I'd have to decide against him. I'm taking a day or two vacation."

"I hope the vacation will do you enough good to counterbalance the loss to us in your leaving the case, Judge", I responded. Not merely diplomatically. I was bitterly disappointed, for I had read many Opinions of this Judge and relied on his keen insight and unprejudiced fair-mindedness. I looked on him as another Dickinson.

An Appeal hearing is a flat proceeding like a cooked meal re-cooked. None of the witnesses are heard and appraised, as in the main trial, nor the incidents seen and experienced, as there. The atmosphere of the trial is lacking. In Judge Dickinson's Court room everyone on both sides felt the defense had miserably crumbled. They had tried to kill our steel with talk, which had fallen as a dead dud.

On the trial, not one lawyer had questioned us why we hadn't put Colonel Curchward on the stand. Had they done so, we would have put in testimony of it, and fought the issue. But after the verdict, rumors went around Steel that much capital was to be made out of it. How could they? How could anyone raise an issue on Appeal that hadn't been raised on trial? Don't ask me. It can't be done. But it was. The presiding Justice raised that very issue himself. Our Counsel explained frankly why, and the Judge seemed satisfied and indifferent, but he raised it again in his Decision of the Appeal.

They had a special lawyer argue this Appeal for Biggs Mill. He argued the case along his own impressions and it didn't seem to match at all with the issues which had hung heavy in Judge Dickinson's Court. He pooh-poohed this and minimized that, and smoothed over much that was bothersome to him. You would never suppose he knew that the Steel had gone through the heaviest ballistic tests to get adopted by Government, or that anyone had given the old steel to the Navy without telling them they had "abandoned " Churchward steel. All the real issues of the trial faded, and his views swung from this to that on free lines.

This is the weakness of Appeals. No one hears the case as it was, as it developed and was fought. Judges read cold words, listen to new talk from lawyers, and either feel the Deciding Judge was wrong and the Appellant right on some law point or other, or else they feel the Judge was quite right and the Appellant "all wet". Depending upon how the arguments and personalities of two Appeals lawyers swing the Judges.

When the Biggs lawyer attacked Judge Dickinson's verdict, he climaxed his criticism with the bold statement that he just couldn't understand how he reached that decision "unless the Judge was hypnotised" . There was a mild murmur and sensation in the Court room as he said this, and all the Judges turned and looked at me. Had they heard this slander of Steel against me? Why had they looked at me?

I met their gaze unconcerned, but when my eye

met that of the Biggs lawyer as he tried to glance at me not too baldly and barefacedly, I smiled an amused and slightly pitying smile at him. He reddened, hesitated, and hastily added, "hypnotised, that is, I mean, by the $20,000,000 that was sold of this steel, and the $275,000 that was paid the Churchward Company for settlement."

The Appeal was decided against Churchward and Judge Dickinson's verdict reversed completely. The patents were declared invalid and void. Not only was the whole "state of the art" outlined unfavorably to the old Colonel's inspired solution of what had bested the best minds of Steel, bit it was stated that no steel could be patented unless it made a new alloy especially useful. The "preponderance of evidence" was that our steel had been tried for Government use and "abandoned " as not good. If not useful, then not patentable. Invalid. Void.

The Colonel's invention was smashed, his patents wiped out, his steel stigmatized as no good. It had passed all tests, and been used extensively. Projectiles hadn't been able to pierce it, but words had. $20,000,000 had been paid for it by Uncle Sam. None of it had come back. None of it failed. None of it was brought into Court and shown with any defects or flaws. No man who ordered its "abandonment" came into Court to prove its badness. It had been abandoned two weeks after buying it up so no one else could sell it to Uncle Sam. Carnegie's lawyer had asked for more of it. They had sold it still for especially necessary points to protect on ships.

In a million autos a million gears of Churchward steel were turning. The very judges who decided this appeal may have stepped from Court into cars whose gears were made of this great steel.

Such is Justice. Such is Law.

The Judges did not specifically decree that this steel was no good. Just that in the case where it had been so sworn, the "preponderance of evidence" had been thus. In Law, words are weighed on each side of the case. These Judges found the words against Churchward steel preponderant over those in favor of it. Not that the fact must be so, but their interpretation of the scene staged was that more weight was spoken against it than for it.

In the battle of lawyers they found that the opposing lawyers either had a better case or had made out a better case than the Churchward ones. You and I, and many who knew the facts, view this from a fairer angle. But Law and the Courts are not perfect instruments of Justice. Law has established a system of fighting suits, which seems to many a fencing match of lawyers, with the Judges as referees.

Judge Dickinson saw an honest cause, sought by shrewd lawyers to be befogged by words to his befoozlement. He saw Right, and could only decide for the Right. The Appeals Court saw it differently from him.

But suppose they were wrong and he right. Was there no redress to be had? I will show what might have been done, but our system of jurisprudence and Government would not permit to be done. Right died under Law's blow.

XI.

THE NAVY, JUSTICE, AND WAR DEPARTMENTS PLAY PUSS IN THE CORNER WITH CHURCHEY AND ME

CHURCHEY WAS ABSOLUTELY BROKEN IN SPIRIT and crushed. He denounced Steel and the Courts. All in it. Also the lawyers and his backers. And myself.

We were really shocked at our debacle. We hushed Churchey up as best we could, telling him it was all nonsense that anyone could buy, fix or influence the Court. They just saw it differently from Judge Dickinson.

Our Counsel prepared an application for a Rehearing of the Appeal, pointing out to the Court the facts again, the overwhelming evidence of the vast value, the Navy tests, the long use of Churchward steel, and the palpable and flimsy nature of the testimony about any socalled "abandonment", the absence of any proof brought into Court of any bad steel, or any rejection by the Navy or anyone else.

They refused to rehear it. We then went to the Supreme Court of the United States. Requested a review, the right to appear and show the Supreme Court injustice had been done.

Originally in our Federal system, the right to appeal to the Supreme Court against a wrong decision of a local Federal Court was inviolable, where reason existed. But influential men in recent history had altered the arrangement of appeals, so that today the Supreme Court will not hear any appeal unless it thinks some important principle of Law is involved, or a Constitutional question, or the rights of a State or the Government, or where Federal Courts in different Districts have decided the same matter two conflicting ways.

On cases simply of wrong decisions, where the Appeals Court was wrong, where some injustice seems to have been done, the decision claimed to be contrary to right, the Supreme Court will not ordinarily bother.

The result of this is that if in any State the Appeals Judges, endorsed and appointed at the behest of the party leaders of that State, decide a case wrong, there is no redress. If these Judges are party men who have either been lawyers for Big Business or been backed po-

litically by the influence and contributions of Big
Business to the Party, if they are rich men who have
inherent trends to favor Big Interests and disdain those
on the outside looking in; then it makes little difference
what the Judge Dickinsons decide in cases they hear; the
Appeals Courts are practically supreme.

I do not refer to this Churchward case, which
I always assume was decided on its merits as best the Court
could see it. I am speaking of the advantage or disadvantage of the system we have. If the party bosses in any State have the
right Judges on the Federal Appeals bench for cases which
seriously challenge Big Business, judges who lean the way
they do by like viewpoints, or judges who will listen to
"the real inside dope on that case, Judge, as I happen to
know" , or who will discuss with some great leader who has
made them judge," Must my client settle with these fellows,
Judge, I hate to advise this when I know our side is right,
but if I'm wrong about this, I'll tell them to shell out";
then the need for some check on the supremacy of Appeals
Courts is obvious.

We supposed that where the Government had
been sold $20,000,000 of Churchward steel for Navy use, and
the defense had alleged that they could use the steel as
long as they liked, but their dropping it proved its badness, the Supreme Court would have considered it. If that
defense was good, then the steel on our warships was bad.

If the steel was good and safe, then a small business had been smashed wrongfully.

In what other country in the world would its Supreme Court refuse to hear a case of that sort ? Our Supreme Court did so refuse. But it did decide to hear a case to settle the grave question whether a candy-maker could put a small prize of negligible value in his candy package.

There are many more serious matters and angles than those I have told here, which call for some reform in the U.S.Supreme Court. I do not personally approve the exact measures proposed in early 1937, having better proceedures in mind. But there was and still is need for remedying and improving conditions variously complained of in that Court by thinking men.

In this, as in all matters herein, I make no reflection on anyone, assuming all men mentioned have and do act from the same motives of what they deem right as I claim to. Perhaps, for aught I know, more so.

Meanwhile came up a strange coincidence. As the sea brings up from the deep things supposedly consigned to its perpetual oblivion, came up hidden facts. Bashford Dean, Curator of Armor of the Metropolitan Museum of Art, (few know there is $15,000,000 of armor there) (owned over $1,000,000 of it himself) the greatest authority on armor in the world, was a friend of my young son who was an enthusiast on armor. Bashford Dean sent him a copy of his work on Armor and Helmets. In this book, among other things, Dean told how he and others had been appointed to test all steels for helmets during the War. They had tested N C V steel, and found it gave such remarkable and superior results, that a large quantity of the steel was ordered, to be used to make further tests.

The member of the committee who was the steel expert ordered to make these tests of N C V steel in quantity, was the same Expert Harris (as I call him) who had testified long after that for Biggs Mill, and sworn that N C V steel was undesirable. Also that it had not been tested for helmets or war material by the War Department and found highly valuable, as I had understood, and he had said nothing about Bashford Dean's and his testing of N C V and ordering a large quantity for further tests, as it had turned out such good results.

When I showed Bashford Dean the testimony of that Steel Expert Harris, he was incredulous. Harris wouldn't say such a thing after seeing the resistance of N C V to bullets. Dean would see Harris at once and get a copy of that later report, which Dean remembered was filed with the War Department and showed N C V steel the only one to employ for helmets.

He did. Harris "did not quite recall all the facts," but would look up the papers. Dean said Harris was much disturbed over the matter coming to light. In a few days, Harris died. Dean was mystified. He was sure Harris would have explained things and made them right. "What puzzles me is, how could he have made such a mistake after our deciding N C V was the steel to use? However, Griffith, that report is in the War Department. I will myself write Colonel Blank to get it for you. You write him too and use my name."

I did. Many times. I also had someone see him. The Colonel was always going to get after someone to unearth that report. At last he sent it to me. It was not the report at all. "Why that" said Dean, " is an older report of quite another steel we found inferior to N C V. I'm sure, if he looks further, Colonel Blank will find the right one."

The Colonel never did. The archives and pigeon-holes of the War Department hide many things that never see sunlight. Then Dean got me the name of the people who had furnished all the N C V steel to his committee and filled the new large order. I applied to them for the truth, and they referred me to Mr. Soandso of Washington for permission to tell me. I found this was a man affiliated with the Inner Circle of Steel. Needless to say, he "knew nothing of the matter, but was sure I could easily get it from...
...... Colonel Blank of the War Department ! "

Through friends Churchey had appealed to the Navy Department to intervene in this matter in some way, and aid him by proving that the Government had never rejected his steel, never found it no good, and still thought they were getting it. High authority investigated and decided they would like to find out how they could be sold steel for $20,000,000 that was "no good" . Would like their money back if that were so. They referred Churchey to the

Department of Justice. They wanted this branch to get all the facts. At once.

An Assistant Attorney General asked Churchey for an orderly statement of facts. Churchey came to me. Asked me to go to Washington and file complaint. I had no faith in it. Steel would learn of it, and we'd be given the run around for my pains. But the Justice Department said it was really interested. An Assistant Attorney General came to New York to meet me at the office of a relative of the Patent Counsel of the Navy Department, and urged me as a citizen and patriot to help him. He wanted a statement of everything we claimed had been done, in such form that every sentence was indexed with a reference to some testimony in the case to prove it.

I spent two weeks, days and nights, on this, and gave it to him in person. He went over it. "Good ! You have done us a big service. We shall see that your case is reopened on motion of the Attorney General. Then we will have the Navy Department bring all its evidence. We will have a showdown. Either this steel is what it was represented to us, or we shall demand a refund of $20,000,000. If it was good, we shall demand that they resume supplying us with this fine N C V steel, and on such proof that the steel was good, the Court will of course have to revoke its decision against you."

This looked excellent. The mercurial Churchey was in the highn heavens. Again I was "the only man who could have saved us, Perc. The Attorney General told me he hadn't expected such a clear and convincing statement of deadly facts quoted from the record. He says those boys will have to fish or cut bait; either give back the money if the steel was bad, or he will make them prove it was good and as represented and save our patents."

What happened? Weeks passed. I got disturbing reports from sources in one of the departments.....it is easy to guess how, from the foregoing.....that all was not going well. Finally the Department of Justice sent me a nice report that they found the goods were sold to the Navy Department, so unless the Navy made a complaint, they could do nothing. If they requested the Justice Department to act, it would.

The Navy Department after long delay, rendered a **solemn** decision that since the Justice Department had found no reason to do anything with all the facts before it, it wasn't for the Navy to do what the Justice Department decided not to do.

Spenlow and Jorkins. Puss in the Corner. The old Scotch custom of Hunting the Gowk. I had spent months on this chase of the will o' the wisp of justice, in the three departments of War, Navy and Justice. Had "heard much talk about it and about, but evermore, came out by the same door that in I went."

Churchward patents and Churchward steel were dead.

Churchey was naturally blue and nerve-shot. He blamed everyone. That there was Wrong, proved to him there was Someone who had done the wrong.

He wished me to take up the sale of his other steels. Made with cheaper alloys of molybdenum or titanium. This I could not do. If this superb N C V steel could be beaten up in the Courts, I had no faith in any steel patent. I had learned much of the inner workings of Steel. I had been inside and established friendly relations and arranged large contracts and made a name and standing that got me into any Steel President's sanctum. But with N C V discredited, my plumes were trailing in the mud, and my prestige was gone.

There was one avenue of hope left, which I essayed, but it came to nothing. My friend Dinkey had gone to Montana and Wyoming hunting, and sent me a picture postal card from there. I wired him of the decision upsetting the patents and he wired back asking me to meet him in New York on his return.

He was helpful in discussing it while we were trying for a review of it by the Supreme Court. After this failed, we discussed his coming out with a sworn statement telling the true facts about N C V steel as he knew them, and asking the Court to reopen the case because he personally knew injustice had been done. Bashford Dean agreed in that case to tell what he had found in his tests of it for helmets, and how "Harris" had been ordered to make wholesale tests of it.

We also discussed my prosecuting suit against Dinkey's Midvale Company, which had made some of the steel. This would be thrown out on the decision upsetting the patents already in the Biggs case, but if Dinkey admitted in his Answer the truth of our claims, we could reverse that verdict. Of course we would not collect damages against them, or settle for a no**m**inal sum. [*would* inserted above]

He asked me to meet him and his Counsel the able, wise and **prominent** Judge Wintersteen at Philadelphia. Wintersteen discussed it quite frankly with us, but after we had gone over all the angles of the case, he counseled Dinkey not to intervene.

S**o** far Churchey and I had continued friends. We had had a rather long discussion of Mu, to which I shall refer hereafter in its due order, which had strained things a good bit between us. I had gone into the facts about Mu, and his writings and conclusions about Mu, rather **definitely, which may have made him feel I was against him on some phases of it I shall refer to later, but we had come to an understanding, at least at that time, about some essential features,** points and angles of that interesting subject.

But one day he came to me with a bright idea. Harkins (as I call him) of Biggs Steel Company (as I term it) which had killed Cock Robin, the patent**s**, came up for election to membership in one of the most prominent organizations of business men in the whole world. Of this I was and am a member for many years, since I was a young man who had reached business standing early. One other man interested in Churchward Steel was also a member and he would oppose the election of Harkins, if I would get three more members to join him, with my own vote. Five adverse votes of members at the monthly meeting would kill the Harkins nomination for a year, and if he risked trying again, we **could** repeat the dose.

Could I get these three others? I could but I certainly wouldn't. On the contrary I would see the other member already committed to blackballing Harkins, and change his mind. I had never met Harkins, I told Churchey, and didn't know his motives. He might be as cocksure he was right as we were. He might simply have done as Briggs, the founder of that Company, wished. He might really know little of the truth of the case.

The Colonel was black with anger. "You dare to defend what they did? You won't aid me to punish this blankety blank as he deserves? What sort of a friend are you anyway, when a man is crushed and needs your sword?"

"I never judge any man unheard," I answered, "I have myself too often been the victim of false beliefs about me, things I am, or have said, or have done, accepted without hearing my side, by persons who, when they did get the facts, were ashamed of their credulity. Who hasn't? This man Harkins no doubt regards you as a freak inventor intruding in Steel with nothing new in your craw, and me as a dangerous interloper and first-class mischief-maker, both of whom it was a pure duty to crush."

Churchey sneered at this idealism. "You know what they did, and what they robbed us both of, and what they did to their own Government. Was that fair? When you won that verdict of a million, Steel went around claiming you had hypnotised the Judge, just as you had Linthicum and Dinkey. On the Appeal, they had the audacity to utter the same thought guardedly. Do you call that fighting fair, any of it all?"

"Have it your own way, Churchey. I don't attribute wrongful acts to any one man or concern, until I have proof as to him or it individually. In corporations, the separate routine acts of various people, each doing what he is told or thinks correct to do, often sums up an injury to someone. A Nation often does wrong in history, but each statesman or official or captain did what he thought was right and in his line of duty. An enemy is an enemy to be fought. As for any blackballing Harkins behind his back, it would be such a public blow to his prestige that it would hurt him and all his family. I don't fight that way, and will see that this other member does not do such a thing or get anyone else to."

I did, and the thing was dropped. Harkins was duly elected. Steel might fight me undercover, but I don't and won't. I don't deliver blows from ambush that cause any man mental anguish. But Churchey thought I was too easy with his foes. Steel had won me over to its ideas with its snaky charm. I was bamboozled by the rich villains who had hamstrung him. I was, in fact, a turncoat and a traitor.

Before our scene ended, he smiled, took back his harsh words, said I was just too much the English gentleman to handle these Yankee Steel crooks. But he was sore at me for it, as he was for my disagreeing with him about aspects of the Mu problem. He left me with the hope that I would yet find some way to reopen that steel case and win him justice. While my time was taken with many other interests and business and researches of my own, he knew that I would never let go on N C V if I ever saw an opening to do anything further.

Some time before, certain financial men interested in Churchward steel, finding no new and large returns from that, since the $275,000 settlement, made me a remarkable proposition. These people or their associates owned an old and valuable franchise. It was their bright notion that a well-known statesman in the Cabinet could have the Government proceed with a large improvement undertaking which would be of high necessity in time of any invasion during a War. To do so, would necessitate the Government acquiring by purchase or condemnation the franchise of these financiers.

The proposal was that the Government should pay them $5,000,000 for this franchise. Of this they would pay me one half, $2,500,000, of which I would agree with the Cabinet official to employ $2,000,000 to back him for the Presidency of the United States, for which he had aspirations; the remaining $500,000 would be my own share, together with any political privileges and preferment I could secure as part of the bargain.

While I had never met the statesman, I had once done him a favor through his representatives, who would have brought me in touch with him gladly. But of course there was nothing I could consider about this proposal. I added that if I were willing to lend myself to it, the statesman would heave me out of his office or send for the police. They accepted my own refusal but cynically doubted my appraisal of the politician's reaction.

An odd element of the interesting proposal was that while Churchey was the last person they would trust with such a secret and private matter, and bound me never to disclose it to him, which I never did, Churchey came to me and told me all about it. I could not ascertan how he learned it, and when I asked the parties, they were astounded that he knew it, and somewhat frightened.

When I told Churchey I had rejected the offer, he nodded and endorsed my attitude warmly at the time. But now, after Steel and the Courts had, he felt, gypped and rooked him, he reverted to this, and mourned that I had not taken the proposition. "Think what a position you'd have been in to overturn this wrong decision! It seems to me, Perc, that in America anyone and everyone can play as crooked as they like against me, but you can't do the least thing off the line against them in return. All my life here I've been too scrupulous in a country where everyone else gets away with murder, rape and wholesale larceny."

Of course with a certain type of person I run the risk, in narrating this experience, of being suspect of a story to which the large amounts involved and the Warwick role, lend a color of implausibility. I do not know what to do about that, however, unless I omit this and some other facts of a truth stranger than much fiction; and I prefer to state all the actual facts with complete unconcern in this volume, "regardless"..

XII.

SENATOR COLEMAN DU PONT INTERVENES .... PRESIDENT HARDING, SECRETARY DAVIS AND JESSE SMITH.

IT WAS FOR SOME YEARS my custom to spend part or all of the Winter months on the East Coast of Florida, the American Riviera. I knew many prominent people there. In Miami Beach, I suppose I knew everyone known. Among them, to indicate the wide extent of influx to the Summery-Winter paradise, were three who had been candidates for the Presidency on the Democratic ticket, James M. Cox, William Jennings Bryan, and Alton B. Parker.

All of them capable men. Jim Cox of Ohio, had a home across the way from my house at Miami Beach on North Bay Avenue, near the Nautilus Hotel. I had much delight from the fact that my giant palms, transplanted by machinery and twelve men, flourished while his wilted. Not that I wished him any hard luck, but his had been laid down by a costly landscaping organization at many times the expense of mine, and there was a bit of honest rivalry there. Cox inquired the reason. I told him, "You and your people were still sound asleep mornings when I, rising with the sun, tunred on a stream of water flooding each tree till breakfast time." Cox is an incessant inquirer, who draws from each man all he knows. I was with him three days on a coastwise ship and felt I had been drained dry mentally. To balance this, Cox is a mine of information, and one who knows him intimately will marvel that his presidential campaign did not fully reveal him in his true stature.

Alton Parker was no Wealth-Soaker, just a fine judicial Jeffersonian, a trifle small-town. He told me that after his nomination he questioned whether Senator Hill had glossed over Parker's strong gold views. Had the nomination been won fairly ? (I knew that when Bryan asked Hill about Parker's **stand** on **bimetalism**, Hill answered "I don't know" as Bryan told me so.) Parker, on his morning ride on horseback, was disturbed. "My horse, Griffith, seemed to share my doubt, and as I dropped the reins idly over his head, he turned his steps toward the telegraph office. I did not consciously direct him. He stopped at the office there. I dismounted and sent that famous telegram, which I think would have elected me if the election had been held that week. Anyway, my horse did it."

Bryan I met a number of times but was not

intimate with him. He felt himself alien to Floridian Winter tourist levity and gayety. He had to wink at heavy drinking and bootlegging under his eyes, even at affairs he attended. Also at openly run gambling houses. He knew, he told me, he would become a hermit there, or have to leave, if he tried to do anything about these things. While in sympathy with much of Bryan's viewpoints on scoial justice, I felt he had too many mistaken ideas. His conduct of the State department, his errors on the silver question, his religious provincialism, his silly attitude in the Evolution case, his ignorance of science, of the very bible he espoused, of the subject of science on which he wished to enforce his wrong views, revealed him as too narrow and generally wrong-thinking. He might have been a force for much good to the plain people, with more knowledge, more breadth of mind, and better judgment.

Senator Coleman Du Pont was one of those I knew well and esteemed highly. In a proper system of social and financial and industrial equity, such a man as Coleman Du Pont would have left a permanent and powerful and beneficant impress on his times. (As would my good Parisian friend Grand Duke Boris of Russia if the Bolshevists had known enough to elect him Leader of a New Russia instead of kicking him out of it.)

When Coleman Du Pont was not engaged in a business deal, he doffed his wealth as one takes off an overcoat, and was a delightful companion. Genuinely liked for himself, he was jolly and good-hearted, and popular, whether your other guests were young or old. He possessed an immense fortune. He told me once, "If I died a resident of Delaware, it would cost my heirs $6,000,000 more than for me to die a resident of Florida."

He introduced me to many statesmen who came down to the Miamis. President Harding, Labor Secretary Davis, various Senators. (Also the inimitable Evalyn Walsh McLean, who in a sea-green panne velvet swimming suit breasted with me the roughest surf I had ever gone into at Miami Beach, and stuck it out laughing, indomitable.)

Harding had already begun to show the strain of office. He looked as if he smoked too much, sat too much, was under too many pulls and pressures from demanding interests. His death a few months later was almost a foregone conclusion. He died from the job as Senator Philander Knox feared he himself would have. Knox's timidity made Harding President....hence Coolidge too. When Frank Lowden and Leonard Wood had deadlocked and talked each other out of the race, the Boies Penrose clique, in the saddle, turned to Knox. They got his friend Cyrus Woods, later Ambassador to Spain and to Japan, to approach Knox. Knox said if he could be renominated for Senator he would refuse to run for President. Penrose was horrified. "Why, it's equivalent to election this year ! No man can refuse the Presidency of the United States ! " Knox then confided his reason. He had heart disease and feared he wouldn't survive the campaign. Justly, as he died six months afterward. Then the Presidency was given to Harding, whom it killed slowly. These facts I knew at first hand from Ambassador Woods to me.

When Coleman Du Pont introduced me to President Harding at Miami Beach, on a visit to him purposely short because of illness of Mrs.Harding, the President and his wife were stopping at one of the cottages attached to the Hotel Flamingo, where I stayed before my home there was built, and after I disposed of it. Though he was worried over his wife, he was jolly and most cordial. We had planned to say little, and nothing serious, so I told him a story which was new to him.

Just before the Presidential visit , weeks before, Governor Cox, who had been his opponent in the Presidential race, came to stay at the Flamingo. His advent had been heralded by widespread publicity. Only three years before, millions of his pictures had flooded every hamlet and town in the country. He reached the Flamingo at midnight, and next morning came down early for breakfast. I greeted him, having met him before up North, and we walked to the hotel desk, where Cox said Good morning, genially, and asked for his mail.

"What name,please? "inquired the brilliant clerk. Luckily Carl Fisher and Landlord Krom weren't there to hear him. Cox was so surprised he could hardly reply, but grinned when the young clerk nearly toppled over at his boner. A big

Cleveland Steel Executive, Black Republican type, took me aside to gloat over it. "Wasn't that priceless, Griffith? It paid to get up early this morning. I wouldn't have missed that for anything." He chuckled wickedly at Cox's reception.

When I told this mild episode to President Harding, he and Du Pont also laughed roundly. But Harding nodded emphatically when I said Cox was a very well-informed man and his campaign had not revealed his able statesmanship fully.

Labor Secretary Davis, like myself of Welsh ancestry, was then almost the most popular Republican in America among labor men and professional politicians. His remarkable voice thrilled everyone as we stood together in the Flamingo corridor while he sang an old Welsh song, whose words I did not know, so couldn't join him.

Senator Coleman Du Pont interested himself in Churchward Steel solely through friendship to me, and by an odd chance. He introduced me to four Senators, Hale, Frelinghuysen (whose lovely young daughter was a superb dancer and of a sweet, ingenue, quietly princessly reserve guarding a rare and charming personality) and two others, as "My friend Griffith, who's been down here five months in this Paradise living on his money while we froze and worked in Washington; don't you wish you were he, the lucky dog?"

Du Pont knew I was not wealthy but I felt I ought to disclaim what he said, after we were alone. "Yes, I know, Griffith, but I thought you had interests in Steel, as I heard a lot of you there", he replied.

I explained to him how my big Steel pyramid had been built up and torn down. Du Pont was very much concerned, and questioned me about every phase of it. He undertook to intervene. "Why Harry Daugherty is Attorney General, and will be down here this Winter I think. You must meet him. We'll get it all reopened and straightened out. They can't do this to any friend of mine. President Harding as you know is at one of the cottages of your Hotel, I'll take you over to see him. Don't talk steel to him. Say little or nothing on anything. Mrs. Harding is sick. Jim Davis was a steel puddler in his youth, he knows Steel, and can help us. Nothing to Jim yet about it. But Jesse Smith you know....."

I had met the mysterious Jesse through Du Pont, and had introduced him to many people he wished to meet, and many nice women and girls, which pleased him mightily, as he was that not uncommon being, a man shy with women, unused to them socially, yet with a keen eye for those of breeding and standing. Smith was the puzzle-man of Washington. An intimate friend of the President and the Attorney General, he was credited and debited with much that was not proven. For the fantastic stories put out by sensationalists about his death, there is of course utterly inadequate evidence.

Smith was a plain middle-aged business man, with a paunch, who was said to have prospered as a storekeeper, and looked the part. Two New York women of self-importance socially who met him through me on the beach, disdained to engage him in conversation. "Who was your undistinguished fat friend?" they inquired afterward. "Only the famous Jesse Smith, who came down with the President, " I replied. "If you don't know of him, where have you been wasting your life? " They were keenly disappointed. "Why on earth didn't you let us know he was that Smith? "

"Jess is your man," Coleman Du Pont continued. "I'll get him going on it. Then you tell him the whole story yourself. He'll fix things at Washington for you if there's any fix in them. Why, he and Harry Daugherty are so close they live together at the Wardman Park. Anyway, you know all about that."

I did. The gossip....or information.... about Jesse Smith's influence and his exercise of it, still lasts in men's memories. It is not for me to speak of anything not coming within my own knowledge. If Du Pont could get Smith back of me in N C V steel, Smith could **presumably** get Daugherty, The Attorney General. Let him step into the suit between Churchward Steel Corporation and this Biggs Mill, in behalf of the Government which had bought and used the steel, and tested it, and the case was reopened and as good as reversed.

Senator Coleman Du Pont had the most generalized, erudite and esoteric viewpoint upon Steel of any man in or out of Steel that I ever met. I cannot attempt to quote this view of his verbatim in continuous sequence, for he would say one part of this at one time and another part later. We would discuss it and I would supply a portion, he would say "Quite so," or "That expresses what I was trying to convey the other night." He would utter some part and my answer would supplement it. The following is my resume of it, but the views are mostly his:

Steel is not a lot of factories and mills and furnaces. Steel is not alone an industry of melting iron and carbon and other elements into a new compound. Steel is not making and selling. <u>Steel is a great centralization of power</u>. Power to provide buildings and bridges, rails, machinery. Power to give modern existence to the world, or without its product, take that modern existence wholly away. Power to control the lives not only of hundreds of thousands of employees, but of millions of citizens. Power to control the politics of a State, and even, through that, of the Nation in a close contest. Concentrated Power controlled by High Finance to dictate and direct, to draw from Steel more power to dig deeper their entrenchment in the position of lordship of industry. Steel is one big centre of power that generates and meshes with other centres of power. The railroads; the automobile industry; Aviation; the Utilities; telegraphs, telephones, electric light and heat and energy, gas, turbines. The machinery-making industry. Coming rapidly, radio. And more that you and I don't know are in embryo. All these, and their Master, Steel, are gradually coalescing into one centralized plexus of power-foci, every year more centripetalized together.

Soon it will all be one mass tributary to the Financial Rulers, one vast organon and macrocosm of plants and men and machinery united into a completely integrated National Industry of All Industries. Nominally separate, but intertwined by Finance so that none can operate except in consonance with all, in subservience to the common purpose of a common financial control.

This was his view, though he made no speech, strung his beads on no string. I shall assume responsibility for the words and the continuity, the framing of the entirety, for my share in developing it. All I wish is to give credit to the Senator for his due.... to render unto Caesar that which belongs to a Caesar who was remote congenitally from being a Caesar.

Du Pont had a long talk with Jesse Smith on Steel, and left him with me. "Jesse will get all that dug out for you, Griffith. Let him do it his own way."

Jesse Smith, for a reputedly simple plain shopkeeper, had a clear grasp of the intricacies of Steel, of N C V, and of the whole situation. I did not notice then so much as afterward, that he went right to the core of it all and saw the points and issues involved.

Among his searching questions was this: "Perc, have you enough financial backers to place ample funds at your disposal if needed? "

I was uncertain whether this was facing me with the problem of the political use of money. If so, it would not be the first time, I had been approached. My mind went back to the time I had been asked to offer two million to a Cabinet Officer for his campaign fund.... I had no more intention this time of such a change of my own attitudes than then. I answered: "Jesse, if and when our case is reopened, we have ample funds and authority to pay over <u>any</u> sums I endorse for legitimate legal expenses and retainers."

This seemed to strike the right key-note with Smith. He agreed to go to Washington and consult others about the matter. "If we have no commitments on the other side, Perc, I'll get it opened up and get you justice, don't fear."

It will be noted that he did not say who "we" were. Nor whether the "commitments" were or might be political or based on the merits of the case, or what. It must not, therefore, be assumed that Smith or anyone had any improper influence in mind.

But some days afterward, Du Pont informed me that Jesse Smith found it was impossible to break through the Steel barriers on that case, and if anything at all could be done, it would take time. "Leave it to Jesse; he's a hard man to stop, when he once starts. And he's a damn good friend of yours, which is a big factor." Jesse Smith on his return to the social life of Miami Beach, simply told me "The Senator posted you, Perc. But you wait. I'm not through with those fellows yet. There's a lot to this thing, I've found."

Shortly afterward Jesse Smith died from a pistol shot, supposedly self-inflicted. Reason not stated. Several persons, for their own purposes possibly, ventured supposed explanations of his act which were about as eerie and weird as if I were to hint that someone high in Steel shot him, or had him shot, because he had just previously shown an intention to uncover some N C V steel matter. Needless to say, no one ever was silly enough to spring that as an element of his death mystery.

Steel does not do such things. Big Business does not do them. High Finance does not do them. Not in America. Churchey's obsession that someone had tried to murder him in a big mill by spilling a few tons of white-hot molten metal on him, was too grotesque for credence. You cannot discuss things like that with people who credit them, always without evidence.

As to Jesse Smith, he was outwardly a plain business man affiliated with some official work in some quasi-official or non-official capacity. He was frank, jolly, inclined to be silent and loquacious by turns, and seemingly actuated largely by a wish to be friendly and to be liked. I can add no word to the many things said since his death, questioning his status.

While Smith was in Washington, I received a characteristic wail from Churchey. Being greatly interested in tennis, and wishing to do something for the Miami Beach which had so cordially opened its arms to me, I gave a large silver cup designed by Udall & Ballou and known as the Griffith Challenge Cup, which has been played for by the leading **tennis** ers of the Nation at Miami Beach tournaments. This Cup was pictured in the rotogravure sections of the metropolitan dailies and caught Churchey's eye.

He wrote me asking if, rather than spend my time and money in promoting sports in Florida, I would not be better engaged in trying to get him justice in some way, or helping him introduce his other steels. I replied briefly that at this very moment I was working in high channels in his interest, and would let him know if anything came of it, but not to hope too much, because all roads in this labyrinth always seemed to end at the entrance gates.

This I believe was the last letter I had from my old friend Colonel Churchward, and I did not see him after that. I heard of him through friends and steel men, occasionally. But it was not until the publication of the Lost Continent of Mu that the old Colonel leaped into the limelight again, and became prominently a personal problem to me upon a perusal of his remarkable work.

XIII.

CHURCHEY TURNS FOR SOLACE TO MU AND THE MAYANS

ALL THROUGH OUR STEEL CAMPAIGNS Churchey's interest in Mu ran like a thread through the fabric of the days. It was always there. There were other things he talked; his titanium steels, his molybdenum steels; his electric furnace; high temperatures in making steel, which all scorned and pooh-poohed but gravitated toward. Fishing, and all manner of scientific and physical questions. Churchey would talk on any subject in the world. Religion largely, being a dangerous radical to the orthodox and hopelessly Old Testament fundamentalist to the Liberal. But ever Mu.

Both in religion and in science his mind had grown and developed in a milieu two generations back. He spoke of forces as substantive things almost, things apart from and applied to matter. The issues his mind viewed were those which had moved men in his boyhood. Then he had been progressive in much, but those issues were long since lost in newer knowledge. Where he had been conservative, his permissible opinions then, had become outmoded, and few cared to debate with him his Creationist theories. It was a bore to most informed persons to have Churchey pour out anti-Evolution arguments in the terms of Bishop Wilberforce and the 1870s.

Churchey was freely inventive of hypotheses to replace the errors of fifty years ago, but forgot that in that half century those erroneous dogmas had been replaced long since by newer thoughts he had not absorbed.

He unconsciously recognized evolution and development where his pet theories required them, but showed the seven centuries of the family's churchwarden function in defending creationist fallacies that even creationists usually evaded sponsoring.

Firmly he espoused the Duke of Argyll's halting proposition in the early Victorian era, that Civilization was created fully developed, sprung full-armed like Minerva from Jove's head, and that all savagery was merely a degeneracy from that created perfection.

To Churchey everything modern had been done before aeons back. Nothing new under the sun. Men of today were no different from men of five millenia past. He spoke of Neanderthal men and Cro-Magnons and Piltdown men, of the Old Stone Age and the Neolithic, he would trace with you the development of boats and ships from a dugout through all the stages to galleys and skiffs, sail-boats, full-rigged barks, paddle-steamers, to Europas and Iles de France, yet he clung to that idea that all was done in a perfect mould first by a perfect creator and a perfect tribe of beings in a perfectly golden age.

  I would lead him to follow the course of man's weapons from the stone and the stick to spears and hammers, clubs, axes, bows and arrows, cross-bows, muskets, rifles, cannon, machine-guns, I would slenderize the stone to an arrow, a bullet, swell it to a cannon-ball, evolve it into a shell, and show him the evolution of the giant complex missile, even the torpedo, from the dull lump of stone. Eagerly, smilingly, he would annex all this as Gulliver waded over and took all the enemy's ships to his side in Lilliput. But soon after would deny that anything evolved or that anything was new and unknown to the ancients if you went back to Mu the motherland.

  Apart from these elements in his conversation, Churchey was informed and a good talker on hosts of current technical and industrial and scientific questions, if you made allowances for his weaknesses on those few other items. He had been in countless sections of earth not usually visited, he knew the Orient well, and what he described was interesting and mostly normally set out.

  Intensely mercurial, of circular depressive and

exalted and elated alternation, the promised ups and threatened downs of Steel colored his attitude toward Mu, as toward all else.

With money in sight, we should go to Yucatan and track down Mu like a fossil beast buried in the deep earth. When fortune waltzed off the stage for a moment, he would collect all his notes and material and put it all out at once in a book which should open the eyes of the world to the mute inglorious Milton and smothered Hampden that even the rude heel of Steel couldn't keep down.

Just before my refusal to blackball Harkins of Biggs Mill, Churchey asked me to go over his matter on Mu, inviting suggestions freely.

We were at his home in Lakeville. Here he had a cosy house newly built for him, a few acres of fields sowed with vegetables, pasture for a sleek friendly cow which gave lavish quarts of rich yellow creamy milk the Colonel drank in pitcherfuls at meals and before retiring. A dock and boat-house, a garage for a small car he drove, and a den lined with more fishing rods and boxes of tackle than any one man could use in a lifetime. And in his last years a remarkably loyal and admirable companion to whom he "affectionately dedicated to my wife" his last volume published before his death; a tribute well deserved by one whose attachment to him was as strong or stronger in dark days as in success.

I read over his draft of the Mu story rather

swiftly. It was a work of fiction, in which the submergence of Mu was dramatized, and the manner of life of the inhabitants of Mu before the disaster was ~~minutely~~ described in minute detail.

When I say that the Colonel had never in his long life written any work of fiction, even a magazine story, and that he was well along in years, it may not surprise one to hear that I did not regard the Colonel's bid for fame as a novelist seriously. I told him so very frankly. "Churchey, the trouble is that a novel calls for a very adept and practiced hand at fiction writing. The professional touch needed to get by a publisher, the critics, and interest the reading public, is a vocation in itself. A green hand will usually turn out something like a mixture of East Lynne, Elsie Dinsmore, Jane Eyre and the Rover Boys. A practiced and experienced writer, and a finished work of modern workmanship, are pre-essential. Now your Mu people act like dummy statues and school-girl heros and heroines."

He was huffy. "It's as good as the slush you have in your magazines and $2 novels. Just more interesting."

I asked him why he sought to work it out in fiction. "Why don't you stick to the factual? You told me you were spending years unearthing the truth about Mu, and you projected serious works on it. If you have any real dope on this subject, Churchey, get it together and I'll go over it with you any time. But stick to facts if you're doing facts. Don't let your fish grow bigger after you gaff him and get him into the boat."

He agreed to turn his attention back to the serious archaeological side of Mu, and discussed with me much of his material. As always when he talked of Mu, and Chichen Itza, the resemblances between the Mayan civilization of Yucatan and those of contemporaneous or subsequeny antiquity, Egypt, Chaldea, India, Burma, Greece, I was carried back to our fireside chats with the Le Plongeons and Churchey in my boyhood home.

"See here, Churchey, isn't this just the same thing as old Le Plongeon told us years ago? Where's the difference?" There was a difference, many differences, as will appear. Churchey was annoyed. "I got nothing at all from Le Plongeon except what I already knew in India."

The Le Plongeons had given me their published books on The Sacred Mysteries of Yucatan, Queen Moo and the Egyptian Sphinx and other volumes. These I had either given or loaned to Churchey when he went in for study of Mu. I referred to this. "Churchey, let me see those old Le Plongeon books I gave you. I'm sure this is all in them." Some of it was, but not all. To my surprise, Churchey said he didn't just know where those books were, it had been so long since he'd consulted them.

He then went into a long statement about Mu, and the little Le Plongeon had meant to him in it, and the much he had garnered from other sources. "Le Plongeon placed the motherland of Mu in the Atlantic Ocean, while I place it in the Pacific."

"Well, is that all? Why do you? As I recall the Le Plongeons' theory, Mu was the supposedly mythical Atlantis of Plato. There probably was an Atlantis, as there probably was a Mu."

"The Troano manuscript, which Le Plongeon told us about, says they came from land to the westward. I hold that means, not land to the west of Europe, but land to the west of Yucatan. So, in the Pacific."

"That sounds very reasonable, Churchey. Your pet bete noire, Darwin, believed that the South Sea islands, or some of them, were mountain peaks of a sunken continent."

"Good ! I wish you'd look up that reference, and send it to me. It's just the confirmation I need." (I did, afterward, send him that reference, but as I remember it, my quotation was of some other scientist who gave Darwin as his authority. In one of his books, the Colonel quotes it from the journalist O'Brien.)

"But then how about Atlantis?" I asked him. "Was that a myth and the Pacific Island true? Looks like Plato and Le Plongeon and history against Churchward."

"Where does history come in?" Churchey knew of traditions and random items collated every so often about Atlantis, I didn't need to tell them to him. "If you mean all the dope ever known about Atlantis, I admit it's a strong case. So I'm conceding Atlantis to Plato and Le

Plongeon. I'm putting it in that Mu was in the Pacific, but Atlantis was in the Atlantic, and was colonized from Yucatan by the Mayans, and also sank. I think it's very likely there was an Atlantis, and am willing to allow it, too."

"Then they both sank? Pacific Mu, and Atlantic Mu, or Atlantis? Isn't that too much of a coincidence?"

" No, I'm sure there was a Mu in the Pacific. When I was a boy I read someone who believed the islands of the South Seas were the tops of a big continent there. Then there was Haeckel, who wrote of the land of Lemuria there, but he spoiled it by believing in monkeys and Darwinism. It's odd, though, that his Lemuria should have Mu as its main backbone or centre. Talk about coincidence! Anyway, if Plato and others say there was an Atlantis, I'm ready to throw in Atlantis. But I won't admit it was Mu, the motherland of man. When I was in India, I heard legends that there had been a land to the east and south, and that's Mu, isn't it?"

Now it will be noted that Colonel Churchward did not then claim he had secret information about this Atlantis. He just threw a sop to Cerberus in conceding it. Nor did he allege anything about confidential disclosures to himself about Mu at all. **He had heard legends.**

I then read the introduction he had written to his romance about Mu. In it he claimed that he had gotten the narrative from old stone tablets in a temple in India. These tablets were written in Mayan, and he had deciphered them as he was an expert in Hindu, Sanscrit, Mayan and many other tongues. I laughed at this in a genial way and rallied him on it. "Well, I know Maori, anyway, Perc," he replied, and added, "Griffith he tengato matau " (Griffith is a high noble person).

But when I quoted to him two Maori proverbs, "Ka heke te war o te kaho"......the water in the cask drops, or briefly that Time flies.....and "Homai ke wahie keiwha pirau te ahi ".....give us some firewood before the fire expires, a sort of Do it now or Gather ye rosebuds while ye may, of the Maoris.... Churchey laughed again and threw up his hands.

"I used to know some of it, but I'm rusty. I used to know some Sanscrit and I still remember a lot of Hindustanee. Those are languages of a different class from Maori altogether, more worthy of study by a man of my kind."

I couldn't help posing him here with the fact that Maori has much akin to Sanscrit, and he immediately volte-faced. "They all have. They all came from Mayan. It may be that Maori is the old original Mu tongue, and all these came from it. Maori is a more primitive language, it hasn't the raffinements that became necessary in the atmosphere of India. The life requirements of the Maori are simpler than those of the Hindu sages. "

It would have been easy to oppose to this his pet fallacy that the motherland of Mu contained all modern culture and more, but I forbore. Half of Colonel Churchward thought in terms of modern science and theory, the other half didn't know what its left hand did, and talked like an early

Victorian theological teleologist. I went back to the romance of Mu.

"If you cut out the fiction, Churchey, and stick to the serious side of your Mu researches, hew straight to the line. In fiction you can have tablets in Mayan, but in science, anyone could kill that by showing you don't read Mayan. Many others can, and would attack you, as they did Le Plongeon for other reasons."

"There was a tablet about Mu in India, I once held it in my own hands," he said. "It was in Mayan."

"How do you know? Mayan characters were a sort of heiroglyphics like Egyptian. They might have meant anything. Who told you what they meant?"

"A priest, a Hindu."

"How do you know he could read either heiroglyphs or the hieratic of Egyptian, Mayan or anything else?"

"I don't. He may have just had in mind the old legend about a land to the south."

"That land might have been Australia, Churchey. Legends are strange things. Sea serpent and unicorn stuff. Though I don't question the likelihood of a sunken island."

Churchey was irritated. "You're the queerest bird. All through my steel fight, everyone was lying and gypping and rooking me, and you insisted I must stick to facts and fight them with kid gloves. All the time I was right and my stuff true, theirs was just the opposite. You have the Yankee idea that everyone else can fake except me, because I'm an

Englishman who oughtn't to give them all the same as they give me and everyone."

The next time we spoke of Mu, he had gone back to his romance, and was sure it would take as a work of fiction. I hated to disabuse him. I might be wrong. It might go. Some publisher might introduce him to a ghost-writer who would rewrite it in a professional style and make it a winner. I hinted that as the only objection I saw; the difficulty of getting by with an amateur style and technique. Somehow my lack of opposition swung him the other way.

"I don't know, I think I'll go at it seriously. It's all there, I might win the whole scientific world to the truth. For it is the truth, you know that, Perc, don't you? "

"Very probably, but I don't regard it as a proved fact of archaeology." I looked at his romance again. He had fairly larded its meat with dissertations of Mu and quotations from authorities supporting his views, and illustrated it with masses of eerie and incongruous fragments of temples and ideographs and symbols. I turned to the introduction. Here he had the tablets elaborated. They were in a tongue I had never heard of.....Naacal. I questioned him about this.

"Oh, I thought that was better. Naacal's a dead tongue no one knows at all. It was spoken or written by the Naacals, the inside sacred adepts and priests of the Mayans who settled in Burma. I got the idea out of one of those Le Plongeon books of yours. It was a find, I just stumbled on it. " Later, he told me quite gravely how he had seen a tablet in Naacal and read it, but when I asked him to write down some of the characters, he laughed and clapped me on the back. "You should never have **left your** patent work. You're a born lawyer. No matter; I think I'll give up the fiction plan, though I hate to let go that tablet in Mayan, I mean Naacal, it's all the same, only more so. **But I see I'd better drop the tablet idea.**"

After dinner that night, he enthusiastically discovered how he could keep his tablets, and his love affair of Queen Moo and Prince **Can**, who were the hero and heroine of his story, though there were an army of other characters brought in without any characterizations or much coherency of their parts in the rambling plot. He had hit on the idea of writing two books, one a serious treatise on Mu for the scientific world and lovers of good literature and belles lettres, the other a romance for the fiction-readers.

"I'll stick to proved facts and first-class authorities, and get you to check it all up for me, and give the kickers no chance. The other I can let myself go....I've thought so long about Mu that at times I almost seem to have **been** there. You know in India they would say I had surely lived there in another incarnation. I saw so much weird inexplicable stuff done **in India**, that I almost believe in reincarnation myself. Could it be that I was in Mu 25,000 years ago, and remember much of it? Perhaps I'm the best authority of all, better than Le Plongeon. He was only in Yucatan in the last century, I was in Mu aeons ago and maybe died in the submergence. That would make it say 13,000 years, about half."

"Good, Churchey! So long as you confine that to your fiction work and don't try to spring it in your scientific volume. Don't think about it too much or you'll get to believe it. Like you always believed your own fish stories after telling them a few score times."

Then we spoke about the Le Plongeons. I went over much of his material and showed him I already knew that from the famous French explorers we had so enjoyed meeting in my boyhood. I found Churhhey didn't recall this as I did, and concluded perhaps he was right, I had magnified the part of the Le Plongeons, in his Mu matter. Things he said he had discovered in other records, might have been as he recalled. But there was a good deal that I was quite sure of, and I warned him about it.

"You must give full credit to these people, Churchey. They started you on the thing, and you have their books. Go over those volumes, and credit to them every inch that belongs to them." He promised to, and meant it. He voiced only one objection.

"If I quote such a lot of this from Le Plongeon, with page and paragraph, quotations of his writings, my book will seem like a mere rehash of something published half a century ago... forty years perhaps... and no one will take mine. Yet I'm right about the Pacific cataclysm, and Le Plongeon with his Caribbean sinking, is wrong, and the world will continue to

208

think like he did. Is that right? "

I told him it was absolutely beyond question that he must make no use of Le Plongeon matter without stating unequivocally where it came from, with volume and page. I selected quite a number of items from his material which I knew definitely had either been printed in the old French explorer's works or told to me by him. Among them was the Cosmogonic Diagram I shall outline later, the Greek alphabet allegedly telling the story of the Mu submergence, a mass of comparisons and resemblances between Mayan mysteries and gods and symbols and those of Egypt, Chaldea, Greece, India, and Burma and Cambodia. These appear in Colonel Churchward's books, but there were a large number of details which he had in his draft of his first Mu book, which he omitted, later, when he came to publish.

Churchey included such items as the Adam, Eve and serpent explanation from a Mayan standpoint, but deleted, so far as I can find, such others as Baal being Mayan for a high chief, Moloch being Mayan Mol, to gather, and och, food....names of gods taken from Mu sources. He had retained the disclosure of Le Plongeon that Prince Can's name had become the widely used Oriental title of a ruler Khan, but deleted references to certain Mayan "Magic Words" and words used in the Habrew bible and the Christian New Testament.

He was ~~using~~ intending to use, but I believe didn't, an interesting explanation by Le Plongeon that after the cataclysm the Mayans started a new chronology based on the number 13, so as to preserve the memory of the day, the 13th day of the month of Chuen, on which the submergence occurred. They had made a week of 13 days, a period of years 4 times 13 or 52 years as we compute 100 for a century; and a grand cycle of 260 years, 13 times 20.

There is here an excellent explanation of how the number 13 came to be regarded as evil and unlucky. Among Christians this is attributed to the number being the group of Christ and the twelve disciples. But that is hardly an evil number nor, if the Christian priests' doctrine that Christ purposely died to save the world from Sin be true, and Sin has thus been eliminated from Earth, is it any cause for fear of 13. Besides, this evil nature of the number 13 antedates all that. If Mu was sunk on the 13th of one of their months, and the Mayans spread their culture and mysteries over the globe, there was ample reason for them to execrate that number.

Churchey in discussing this, made a last bluffing attempt to claim he'd found all that in his Mayan tablet in "Naacal", but when I reminded him that he'd already admitted that the tablet idea was only part of the fictional romance of Mu, and that he would drop it from his serious scientific work on the sunken island, he agreed.

"Of course, Perc, you don't realize that the tablet plan would be a very striking publicity move. In America they demand sensation. Look at your colored Sunday magazines in the newspapers and your tabloids. People here love that sort of thing. And there is good precedent for it. Moses told the Jews that God had given him ten tablets with the ten commandments on them. We all know Moses went off for a few days, and chiseled them out himself. But for thousands of years the world had obeyed them......"

"Disobeyed every one of them ! Merely demanded of everyone else to obey them, or the ruling violators would beat up, jail or burn or hang the subjects violators."

"Yet where would the world be today without those ten commandments...if Moses hadn't faked them for the purpose of impressing the people with the great truth he had to offer?"

"Well, that's all right for Moses, but you'd better lay off pulling any such stunts with tablets telling the contents of your Mu book. People are not so gullible today, Churchey."

"No ? Well, you've been out in Salt Lake City, and seen the Mormon State laid down on the "discovery" by Joe Smith of the Book of Mormon, and the "sacred revelations" made to Joe Smith by God of things told to Moses and Abraham, and not found in the Hebrew bible. Here's a State as big as many ancient Nations, all of whom believe in this Mormon story. If Moses and Joe Smith worked the sacred tablets story, you as a good salesman and promoter ought to see the value of it in my Mu story."

When Churchey saw I was displeased at the revival of the tablet subject, he changed face again, and told me he had no intention of using it, except for a romance based on the submergence of Mu.

We then discussed the Troano Manuscript and the Codex Cortesianus, with both of which he was familiar. We both **execrated** the Spanish Bishop of Landa for destroying all the vastly valuable Mayan books which might throw so much light on the subject today. The bigoted Landa in Yucatan did just what the Mohammedan Caliph did in Alexandria centuries before....."If these infidel books agree with what our Koran says, they are superfluous; if they disagree, they are blasphemous". So the great Alexandrine library went to heat the baths of the Faithful. And the Mayan books were burned to destroy forever the truths they might reveal, by religious zealots who ran true to a form as old as religion.

Churchey spoke of the Atlantis question again. That queer little combination of letters "Atl" so frequent in Mexico and Yucatan, so rare in other languages. Yes, as I pointed out, it came from Atlas. The atlantes or male figures acting as columns were symbols of Atlas holding up the Earth, and Atlas was supposed to come from tlao, bear, in the Greek. But if the Mayans had spread over the earth, maybe that first "atl", old Atlas, came from Mu.

"The Mayans named the Atlantic", he declared, "just as their finger may be detected in thousands of things, once you start looking."

"Yes, Maya was the country, the goddess, the god at times. Its root Ma meant mother, and Maya was mother to all civilizations in giving them the very name of mother common to all of their tongues."

"I'm sure of it, and the Mayans were the first to call Ma the earth; the mother earth that all people term it."

"And the Maypole, survival of the ancient dance around the pole of the Mayans. Churchey, there is no telling how far this research into the early customs of the Mayans may take one, if archaeologists and anthropologists conclude to make a mass investigation of the flow of civilization."

"It will break up a lot of old-time notions".

"For one thing, it is known that Egypt shows no traces of savagery, but its civilization seems to have been all we know of it. Colonization by a superior race is here indicated. If it can be shown that Mu sent her colonies all over the Earth and superseded or formed the dominant peoples of the principal countries, you will have started something of tremendous value to the study of man."

"What worries me, Perc, is the idea that someone will accredit all this to the Le Plongeons. They missed utterly my theory that Mu was in the South Seas. But if I don't watch out, people will think I got that from him, too."

"Yes, but Churchey you must keep in mind that Le Plongeon missed something bigger. He lost the confidence of archaeologists by some too loose or extravagant claims, and Science has not adopted his theories, nor given its seal to his explorations. Don't be afraid of giving credit, be afraid only of making any part of this work a fish-story."

Better review of all Churchey's materials showed so much that was different from Le Plongeon, that he needn't, I felt, fear on that score. "Just frankly state that the base of all this is the Le Plongeon theory and discoveries, his affiliations of the Mayans with a Motherland of Mu, and with all other civilizations which he and you claim grew out of the Mayan. 'There's credit enough for all'....if Sampson had adhered to that early view of his on the Santiago naval battle, the worst modern stain on the Navy escutcheon in the silly controversy would have been avoided."

"The worst modern or other stain on the Navy is the way it let these Steel people take my steel away from the Navy and substitute the old steel bolstered up", declared Churchey, hotly, " and the way they evaded opening it up when you gave the Attorney General all the facts to do it."

To this true comment he added a few strong Devonshire epithets to the various men in Steel who had "gypped" and "rooked" us. "As the Mexicans have said to me, Perc, 'Los Yankeros muchos ladrones '.....the Yankees are all thieves"

"Not to my mind, old man," I replied. "Rather 'Senatores boni viri, senatus malus bestia est '.....the Senators are good men, the Senate is a wild beast. The men in Steel all have been square decent men doing what they thought proper and usual in a fight. Steel in its collective sense of Inside Steel, has been the wild beast."

He couldn't see it. I was too tender to the foe,

they had dazzled me with their highly respectable brigandry. I was, he mourned, no Sir Richard Grenville who would go down fighting:

>   They praised him to his face,
>   With their courtly Spanish grace,
>   But he stood upon their decks
>   And he cried,
>   I have fought for my queen and faith
>   Like a gallant man and true,
>   I have only done my duty as a man
>   Is bound to do.
>   With a joyous spirit I,
>   Sir Richard Grenville, die.

"You lose with a joyous spirit, Perc, but you don't die fighting, and you are too easily charmed by their courtly Spanish grace. But about Mu, I'm going to make them all sit up and admit I'm the same leader in archaeology as I was in Steel until they knifed me in the back."

Later he seemed to have lost interest in the fiction end of Mu, and was completely wrapped up in its research end. We had many chats on it, as we had had for all the years, but I repeat my definite disclaimer, I had no part in his work, except to introduce him to the Le Plongeons and converse with him about various details of it such as these.

After I refused to join in the blackballing of the enemy "Harkins", and killed the plan to do this, Churchey and I drifted apart. There were so many duties and interests in my fairly busy life, he lived far away, he didn't come down to Stamford as he used to, I moved to Westchester. Steel was dead, there was nothing to bring us together. I heard of him occasionally. Bitter remarks about all in Steel, not excluding his own allies. Stories of a new steel, better than any before. Stories that he had written a book but couldn't find a publisher.

I hoped this was true, and that it was his long-loved brain-child Mu. I trusted that his real innate genius had come to the fore, and given us a work worthy of crowning the long career of my old friend Churchey. One doing justice to the great theme he had spent forty years studying.

For in this sunken island of Mu, lie many far-reaching disclosures, if the hypothesis is true.

The cradle of the human race. A race whose customs and culture and colonists may be traced all over the globe, if all the thousands of facts pointing to this are assembled.

An entirely new basis for an entirely new ethnology. Explanations for innumerable problems and minor obstacles in the study of all the civilizations of Man.

The line of penetrations of more primitive peoples by the higher. The clue to many superstitions and rites, legends, traditions, leading from this dominant race. Many such preserved in distorted form in places where transiently triumphant barbarisms have overcome the more intellectual civilization.

The explanation of just what was the factual basis of the Hebraic nonsense of Adam and Eve, the serpent, and Cain and Abel.

The origin of the Noachian flood myth, and the ghastly truth underlying it.

The probable origin of cannibalism among various tribes in the South Seas.

A precious gift to philology, in showing whence

the parent language which produced Sanscrit, and the branching Hindu and other allied Asiatic tongues, the Greek, the whole range of the Indo-Germanic, and possibly means to ally a host of others. Through Maori, one of the languages most near to the earliest Sanscrit, and comparative study, to arrive at that form of Mayan which might have been the exact tongue of Mu.

Through this new injection of previously strange blood into the stream of the study of Man, into ethnology, anthropology, archaeology, to re-cast perhaps the entire plexus of those sciences.

A common basis for all religions of the civilized races of antiquity, and for the analysis of religious ideas and systems.

And more....far more...than anyone could predict or pre-catalog. For if only the wealth of effort of Science generally could be directed into these channels, what one man or two men had cut through the jungle with bare hands and machetes, the army of Science could follow with troops and machinery, roads, autos, railroads, tractors, excavators and all the paraphernalia of its conquest of routes first mapped out to it by its pioneers.

Science had been indifferent to the call of the Le Plongeons, except that it had followed them through Yucatan. I hoped my friend Churchey had risen to his opportunity here and shown the timber of a Moses in leading the thousands through the wilderness to a goal worth while.

And what new impetus would be given to geology, seismology, the study of the formation of continents? How would the sinking of Mu in the Pacific, or of Mu in the Atlantic, or the island of Atlantis there, affect the modern theory of continental drift?

It was about that time, two years before Churchey's first book on Mu, that Wegener put out his study of the drift. Take your atlas or globe, and observe how the Eastern coast-line of North and South America, fit in with the Western coast-line of Europe and Africa. Many have speculated on the likelihood that these two continents were joined in prehistoric times, broken apart by horizontal continental drift. How easily you can push them together on the map, and fit them in conjunction like two pieces of a cross-word puzzle.

There is good geological argument for this theory, wholly apart from the pretty pictorial effect of the map or globe. Wegener puts up quite a good front on his pet thesis.

But then where do Pacific Mu or Atlantis come in? Such a separation would go back to the Upper Carboniferous times or not too much later. Would it leave an Atlantis or a Mu? It wouldn't sink them, as the supposed date of either catastrophe is between 11,000 and 25,000 years ago.

But if Science sponsored the Mu submergence, that would be a factor in considering the continental drift theory. And the drift theory would be a factor in considering the acceptance of Mu.

In any case, it was devoutly to be wished that the Colonel had measured up to the great task and subject he had tackled, if he were bringing his forty years of research out into the world's limelight, and I awaited word of its publication with much interest. Noting with mild amusement as I picked it up in a book-shop, that the old man hadn't sent me a line about it, and fearing from this that he "might he hidin' somethin' from me" in this work of his. In which I was quite correct.

XIV.

A SUNKEN CHURCHEY AND A SUNKEN CONTINENT BOTH EMERGE FROM UNDESERVED OBLIVION

EVEN COLONEL CHURCHWARD'S WORST ENEMY must have granted him some grudging messure of applause when the indomitable old warrior arose from the obscurity into which they supposedly had flung him, and became again a sensation in the world, by the publication of *The Lost Continent of Mu*, in 1926.

Once more the gaze and attention of thousands of the cognoscenti were fastened upon him, and of greater thousands of general readers. Banquo's ghost that wouldn't down. The Phoenix arisen from its own ashes. Literally, a fighting spirit you could not vanquish.

If I say that the Lost Continent of Mu fairly burst upon an astonished world, I do not overstate. Many do not realize the furore it caused. It received wide attention from reviewers and became the subject of much discussion.

The work was elaborately planned and executed. It showed the forty years of research, of writing, copying, drawing, painting, collecting data. There were innumerable illustrations, many listed plates but also quantities of smaller ones interspersed through the text. Ancient designs and symbols, fragments of sculpture and architecture found in many parts of the earth.

There was an immense network of quotations from writers and records of all ages and all kinds. Sages and antiquarians, histories, old manuscripts, modern writers, even current newspapers.

Its style, while distinctly amateur and naive in both literary and scientific senses, was readable and convincing in the main. In a really masterful way he grouped his facts and evidences and arguments, made comparisons, demonstrated resemblances, affinities of objects, manners, customs, traditions of one country and another, all of them of postulated Mayan origin.

He made out a good case for his thesis that the Mayans of Yucatan had come from an ancient and highly civilized motherland called by them Mu; that the cultures of Egypt, Chaldea, Greece, India, Burma and Cambodia were derived from Mayan colonization; and that Mu had, according to the Mayans and other records, been sunk beneath the ocean by a cataclysm partaking of the nature of an earthquake, a volcanic eruption and submergence of the whole land or most of it, with the loss by death of the major portion of the denizens of the motherland.

Had Colonel Churchward rested his case on the firm basis of existing and provable sources of his data, of which he made many quotations, ample for any such work, he might have aroused no scepticism as to his work or himself, and made even more converts than he did; and higher-placed ones.

But he came out with that preposterous pretense, from the outset, that his description of Mu, his story and his knowledge of it, were based upon various stone tablets to which he had obtained access in India from a native priest, which were in an unknown tongue, the Naacal. This priest had taught the language to Colonel Churchward. No man could read it but this priest and other initiates in the sacred mysteries, who had taught it to him.

These tablets Colonel Churchward did not include in his illustrations, nor any copies of them either in the original or in the translated form. Nor would he furnish them and the key to the language to scientists on request. This was so contrary to customary scientific usage, that the author was denounced in some quarters and ignored in others. The very great value of all his collocation of evidences as to Mu, had been diminished by this story of the tablets.

Of course, as I have sufficiently indicated before, there were no such Naacal tablets. The claim about them he had admitted to me was simply pure fiction. It was irrelevant, superfluous, and extraneous at best.

His story in the main was the same as Le Plongeon's. It was what we discussed with the old professor Augustus Le Plongeon and his young wife Madame Alice Dixon Le Plongeon in my home in those early days when I had introduced them both to my friend Churchey, to King Gillette and others.

It was what Le Plongeon had previously published in various archaeological communications to learned societies in parts, had published in 1886 in his Sacred Mysteries Among the Mayans and the Quiches 11,500 Years Ago; Their Relations to the Sacred Mysteries of Egypt, Chaldea, Greece and India. And in 1896 in his excellent Queen Moo and the Egyptian Sphinx. Plus what the Le Plongeons had told us, and supported by photographs, many of them, which we went over with them, as well as monographs by Madame Le Plongeon and her work entitled Queen Moo's Talisman.

But plus also a wealth of detail and new matter Colonel Churchward had worked up in the years following.

Both the Le Plongeons' theories of the sunken Mu and Colonel Churchward's, were based on the Troano Manuscript and the Codex Cortesianus, to which each of them gave full credit, except that the Colonel claimed he had gotten it all from some priest and his Naacal tablets.

Le Plongeon claimed that in Yucatan there were evidences and traditions of the Mu story, and confirmatory evidences in various authorities and records in different parts of the globe, which he quoted.

Churchward claimed the same thing, but with much more detail. He also quoted Le Plongeon in various parts of his book. He did not, however, specifically state that the whole idea of a motherland of Mu for the Mayans, colonizing Egypt, Greece, Chaldea and India, and afterwards sinking into the sea, was Le Plongeon's.

He should have done this, and shown just wherein his differences from that Le Plongeon basis lay. His case and status as an author and scientist would have been far stronger, if he had said:

"This is what I learned from the lips and writings of the Le Plongeons. It fitted in with legend current in India and the South Seas where I have traveled and lived. I have greatly added to the evidences by a mass of material I have worked up. And I depart radically from Le Plongeon in this, that I start from the theory of Darwin that the South Sea Islands are most of them peaks of a large vanished continent, as was the legend in the Orient to which I refer. Where Le Plongeon laid Mu in the Atlantic Ocean, and made it identical with the Atlantis of Plato and other testimonies, I deny wholly that Atlantis was Mu, and allege that Mu the motherland was in the Pacific and is still there today, beneath the waters which submerged it."

This was what the usual proceedure would and ought to have been. It was not followed. On the contrary, the part of Le Plongeon, in spite of many references to him in the Colonel's work, was left diminished, and the whole basis of Mu attributed to some silly mythical Naacal tablets supposed to contain all the story that was the individual contribution of Colonel Churchward to the Mu matter.

Anyone need only read the works of the Le Plongeons to see there the whole story, the main thesis as I have above set it out.

Le Plongeon shows the antiquity of the Mayans, their relations with the cultures of Egypt, Greece, Chaldea, Burma and others. He describes the Troano Manuscript and shows that it gives the origin of the Mayans of Yucatan as being "lands of the West" called Mu. He quotes the Codex Cortesianus, and countless authorities quoted in The Lost Continent of Mu by Colonel Churchward.

The Troano Manuscript, now in the British Museum, was first known in the early part of the 1500s. It is an immense strip of maguey paper which would make a good-sized floor rug for a large livingroom. It is folded like a fan in thirty five folds, so there are about 70 pages of it, completely surfaced with a whitish varnish on which the characters are printed in black, red, blue and brown. Heiroglyphics cover the whole of the 70 pages, and have been deciphered by Mayan readers. This manuscript describes the motherland, Mu, says the Yucatan Mayans emigrated from Mu to Yucatan, and that Mu was destroyed by a cataclysm which submerged it under the waters.

The Codex Cortesianus is a smaller manuscript, believed to be of the same period, found at the same time by the Spaniards in Yucatan, and giving similar details of Mu. Yucatan, by the way, was so named from the natives saying Tectoan (I don't understand) when asked the name of the land. The Spaniards thought this was Yucatan.

Le Plongeon found inscriptions on Yucatan monuments and ruins, showing some of them were memorials to the many in the motherland who died in the submergence of Mu.

He showed that the courting of Queen Moo by Prince Aac, after he had killed her husband Can, was the basis of the Adam and Eve story of Cain and Abel. The serpent, the tribal totem of the Mayans, was in the story, not for the silly reason in the Hebraic account, but because it was the royal totem. The offering of fruit was an act of courtship by Prince Aac, and the refusal an act of declination by Queen Moo.

As Le Plongeon says, the Mayans were the only nation in all history whose ruling dynasty were connected with the so-called Adam and Eve story, with the fruit and the serpent, and the associated Cain and Abel story, both of which the Hebrews wrongly deduced from the picture of the Queen Moo and Prince Aac and serpent episode.

Le Plongeon showed many records and facts indicating the identity of ancient Mu theories and diagrams and figures with those of the other civilizations mentioned.

On the opposite page is a plate showing the Mayan Cosmogonic diagram. This is found on page 17, Plate XVII, of Le Plongeon's Queen Moo and the Egyptian Sphinx.

Now the identical diagram is found in Churchward's Lost Continent of Mu, without any statement that it is copied from the earlier Le Plongeon volume.

Here is Colonel Churchward's explanation of the Cosmic Diagram; which is on pages 140 and 141 of his Lost Continent:

There is a central circle and two interlaced triangles, and an outer circle. This leaves 12 divisions between the two circles. Outer circle is enclosed in 12 scallops. The central circle is Ra. The 12 divisions are the 12 gates of heaven, each gate a virtue. The outer circle is the world beyond, the intermediate world. The 12 scallops are 12 temptations. The ribbon beneath is eight roads man's soul must travel to reach the 12 gates of heaven.

And this is Le Plongeon's explanation of the Cosmogonic Diagram:

In the centre we see a circle inscribed within the hexagon formed by the sides of the two interlaced triangles. The Egyptians held the equilateral triangles the symbol of Nature bountiful and fruitful. Exoterically the central circle represents the Sun, light and heat giver of the physical world, evolved from fire and water. It is well-known that among the ancient occultists the triangle with apex up symbolized fire, and with apex down, water. ********* the outer circle * * is the horizon * * the 12 scallops * * are the 12 houses of resting places of the Sun, that is, the 12 months, of the year, or 12 signs of the zodiac. As to the four double rays * * * direct emanations from the central Sun, the four heavenly giants who helped in fashioning the material universe. The four lower ones symbolize the four primordial substances known to modern scientists as nitrogen, oxygen, hydrogen, and carbon, whose combinations form the primitive elements Fire, water, air and earth.

Churchward neither credits that diagram to the Queen Moo and the Egyptian Sphinx of Le Plongeon, which book I gave him myself, nor quotes the correct interpretation of the diagram which Le Plongeon so carefully gives.

On the contrary, he says that this is the earliest book written by man, and that he has traced it back 35,000 years! There are no records by which Churchey or you or I could trace any writing or diagram back 35,000 years, and in the days when Colonel Churchward was in his prime, before Steel crushed him and shattered him, he would have been the very first and loudest and strongest to back me up in that statement, no matter whom it hit, dear or ever dear to him.

In Plates XVIII and XIX, on pages 22 and 26 of Queen Moo and the Egyptian Sphinx, Le Plongeon shows further how this Cosmogonic diagram appears in the Egyptian and Chaldean records. This is one of his evidences of the spread of Mayan culture from Mu to those other civilizations.

Le Plongeon is rich with other interesting features and details along like lines. One is the explanation of the medieval superstition that you can cure a mad dog's bite by saying the words hax pax max. Magicians so widely held to this that it was attacked by opponents of superstition as ridiculous, if not ungodly. Now, says Le Plongeon, these are Mayan words which prescribe the right course in case of snake-bite or bite of any other poisonous or vicious animal. Hax is a twisted cord, which was used as an immediate tourniquet to shut off the poison from penetrating up into the blood and body. Pax is music, which in olden days was used widely for calming an injured person, and is endorsed by much authority. Max is a wild pepper plant used in Yucatan to lay on wounds, usually chewed up and applied in a moist sticky mass. Being a strong counter-irritant, it draws the poison out of the wound. So it was just a proper prescription of sane and successful proceedure long employed.

I may call attention to two facts. Hocus pocus is a term of medieval origin, of which no one has any authoritative derivation. It may have come from the muttering of hax pax max over bites and other wounds, by magicians and healers who had lost all trace of the meaning of the words they used. There was much of all that in medieval times. Even Bacon hinted belief that if an ointment were applied on the sword or dagger that had wounded one, instead of on the wound itself, it had been known to assist recovery or avert death; not knowing that the antiseptic must be applied to the blade before stabbing with it, not after. The other fact possibly related to hax pax max, is the custom developed in the same times, of invoking the blessing pax vobiscum (peace be with you) in cases of danger or injury. It is not impossible that the Churchmen used that holy expression as a charm to replace and wipe out the heathen hax pax max which had such a hold on the ignorant.

Again Le Plongeon tells us that the words Mene, mene, tekel upharsin, which the Babylonian King found on his banquet wall, and none but Daniel could read, "Weighed in the balance, found wanting", were Mayan words. And that the last words of Christ, Eli, Eli, lamah sabachthani (My God, why hast thou forsaken me?) which no one could find appropriate to a true or soi-disant son of the Deity, were in fact Mayan Hele, Hele, lamah zabac ta ni, meaning "Now, now I am fainting; darkness covers my face." This accords with one of the Apostles recording that he really said "It is finished", which is the equivalent of the last part of the Mayan words.

If it is true that these words were Mayan, and were unknown to the audience, it is interesting evidence that such a man or being as Jesus Christ actually existed, which many have doubted because of absence of his name from contemporary or near-

ly contemporary
authentic histories. Not direct or absolute proof, but contributory, since it would be unlikely for a fraud concocting the narrative, to put Mayan words into his character's mouth, which he could only interpret rather unsatisfactorily.

Le Plongeon gives the story of the Greek alphabet as being the initial words of sentences of Mayan words which perpetuated the memory of the death of the ancestors of all Mayans and offshoots of Mayans, in the disaster to Mu. I give here the chart of Le Plongeon demonstrating how each Greek letter from Alpha to Omega is itself a Mayan word, and how, put together, they describe the Flood of Mu.

Opposite to it, I give the practically identical chart as given in Churchward's Lost Continent of Mu, with no statement that he copied it from Le Plongeon.

I also give Le Plongeon's Free Reading of the flood description, and Churchward's Free Reading of it. This is one of the many things I warned Churchey he was taking from Le Plongeon and must allot credit for.

After a full reading of both authors, what must we conclude as to the facts of Churchward's contribution to the mystery of Mu, as to the statements in his books about how he obtained such facts? And what must we analyse as the motivation of the Colonel in this last connection?

First, as to facts:

1. The entire main basic thesis, that the Mayans came from a motherland of Mu, not only to Yucatan but also to Egypt, Greece, Chaldea, India, Burma, etc., with ample evidences that these various civilizations had much in common, and that this motherland of Mu was submerged with wholesale loss of lives; was published by Le Plongeon a generation before Colonel Churchward's first book, The Lost Continent of Mu.

to face page 214 of Ms

CHART OF GREEK ALPHABET SHOWING MAYAN WORDS AND MEANING

according to Dr. Augustus Le Plongeon.

Greek:	Mayan words, with English meaning	
Alpha	al paa ha	Heavily break water
Beta	be ta	walk place
Gamma	kam ma	receive earth
Delta	tel ta	depth, bottom where
Epsilon	ep zil on	obstruct, make edges, whirlpool
Zeta	ze ta	strike place, ground
Eta	et ho	with water
Theta	thetheah ho	extend water
Iota	io ta	all that lives or moves earth
Kappa	ka paa	sediment break, open
Lambda	lam be ta	submerge go, walk where, place
Mu	Mu	Mu
Ni	ni	point, summit
Xi	xi	rise over, appear over
Omicron	om ik le on	whirlpool, whirl wind place circular
Pi	pi	to place by little and little
Rho	la ho	until come
Sigma	zi ik ma	cold wind before
Tau	ta u	where basin, valley
Upsilon	u pa zi le on	abyss tank cold, frozen place
Phi	pe hi	come, form clay circular
Chi	chi	mouth, aperture
Psi	pe zi	come out vapor
Omega	o mec ka	there whirl sediments

Freely translated:

Heavily break...the..waters extending...over the...plains. They....cover...the..land in low places where..there are obstructions; shores form and whirlpools strike...the...earth with water. The...water spreads on...all that lives and moves. Sediments give way. Submerged is the land ....of...Mu. The peaks..only...appear above the water. Whirlwinds blow around by little and little, until comes cold air. Before where ...existed..valleys...now...abysses, frozen tanks. In circular plains clay formed...a... mouth opens....vapors come forth...and volcanic...sediments.

to face page 214 og Ms

CHART OF GREEK ALPHABET SHOWING MAYAN WORDS AND MEANINGS
according to Colonel Churchward

Greek	Mayan words,	with English meaning
Alpha	al paa ha	Heavy break water
Beta	be ta	walk where, place, plain, ground
Gamma	kam ma	receive mother, earth
Delta	tel ta	deep, bottom where, ground etc.
Epsilon	ep zil on	obstruct make edges whirlwind
Zeta	ze ta	strike where etc.
Eta	et ha	with water
Theta	thetheha	extend water
Iota	io ta	all that lives and moves where etc
Kappa	ka paa	sediment, obstruction break, obstruct
Lambda	lam be ta	submerge, go, walk where etc.
Mu	Mu	Mu
Ni	ni	point, summit, peak
Xi	xi	to rise, to appear over
Omicron	om ik le on	whirl wind place circular
Pi	pi	to place little by little
Rho	la ho	until come
Sigma	zi ik ma	cold wind earth, mother
Tau	ta u	where bottom, valley, abyss
Upsilon	u pa zi le on	abyss tank cold place circular
Phi	pe hi	come mud, clay
Chi	chi	mouth, opening
Psi	pe zi	come out vapor
Omega	o mec ka	there whirl sediments

Free reading:

Heavily break the waters extending over the plains They cover the lands in low places where there are obstructions. Shores form and whirlpools strike the earth with water. The water spreads on all that lives and moves obstructions give way submerged is the land of Mu. Peaks only appear above the waters whirlwinds blow around and little by little until there comes cold air. Before where valleys existed are now abysses cold depths. In circular places mud formed. A mouth opens, vapors come forth and volcanic sediments.

232

2. The account was chiefly based on the known Mayan works, the Troano Manuscript and the Codex Cortesianus, the inscriptions and traditions found by Le Plongeon in Yucatan, and many facts and evidences brought out by Le Plongeon in his books.

3. Colonel Churchward had been introduced to the Le Plongeons by me in my boyhood, and we had all discussed the subject (he states in his books they were dear friends) and I had myself given him Le Plongeon's books.

4. Colonel Churchward's thesis, while so far as above defined identical with Le Plongeon's, departed widely from that in fixing the motherland of Mu in the Pacific, not the Atlantic, and showing or trying to show, that the existing islands of the South Seas are former mountain peaks of an immense continent of Mu. And that if Plato's and Le Plongeon's Atlantis was also existent and also sank, it was only one branch of the Mu race.

5. While a large proportion of Colonel Churchward's references are to authors or records or evidences also mentioned before by Le Plongeon, he added a vast quantity of relevant and interesting quotations and references, which he had spent many years of research to collate.

6. Colonel Churchward's sojourn in India and other parts of the Orient, gave him knowledge of legends and existing material known to archaeologists, which bore on the question, and which he affiliated to it.

7. While Colonel Churchward mentioned Le Plongeon liberally in his work, he did not award adequate credit to him for what Le Plongeon's published books show, and what he drew from them, and what he had learned from his contact with the Le Plongeons.

8. The story of the Naacal tablets must be dismissed as quite unfounded, and a detraction from the substance of the Colonel's large contribution to the subject, not an addition.

Now as to the motives of Colonel Churchward, I have myself no question about them. I see as clearly as I see the character and life of the man, just how his mind worked in this matter of Mu.

I am confidently in hopes that all those who

have read this description of my friend Churchey, his ups and downs, his genius and talents, his unique personality, his bitterness over his really unfair deal in Steel, will see that character and those motives as I do.

If not, it is the fault of my characterization falling below the level and technique of someone better able to portray the man than I am.

I was with him in his life so intimately that my description of him and that life, ought to bring him before you as he is before me as I write. As I weigh him and his acts and omissions, so ought anyone who has read all this.

Even have I, to show you just what is the attitude of the narrator to his subject, what allowances to make on one side or the other for too great indulgence or too great criticism toward my friend Churchey, laid open all our relations, all our dealings, I have sought to place him in a stereoscopic picture, on the stage on which he lived and worked, and figuratively opened up his skull to let you see the workings of his mind in many contingencies and events and incidents.

I believe I have no bias either way, conflicting with a just appraisal. If I have, that bias for or against will itself stand out from my account of us both, of us all who knew him for years.

My conclusion, which I hope will be that of all, is that Churchey studied up Mu so many years, from so many sources, that he didn't in the least know, at the end, how much of his material he had acquired from this source or from that, or when. He was a very old man. Much older than he admitted. And published statements of his age were based on his own statements . His memory was most treacherous and at times shockingly feeble.

The man was shattered by his experiences, by the rise to fame and riches in Steel by decision of the Courts, followed by the crash as the Appeals Court overturned that completely. There was bitterness and hatred in him, and a sense of unmerited injustice.

His mind revolted against seeking altruistically to make gestures of submission to this or that one. He wasn't going to let anyone misjudge and minimize his part in Mu, to which he had devoted forty years, and have the world refuse him a hearing.

He had argued with me about credit to Le Plongeon, and he would do all required. But Le Plongeon believed Mu was Atlantis, and he didn't. He had made a concession to the deceased scientist by putting Atlantis in too. That was enough. As I thought he ought to do more, well, he would.

Churchey threw in references to Le Plongeon in many parts of his book. He never got around to giving him all he wanted to, as I interpret it. He didn't think of saying he had Le Plongeon's books, and going over them with a fine tooth comb to quote each thing of his Mu that ought to be assigned to Le Plongeon.

And what, too, about all that Le Plongeon had told him at my house in bygone days? How could he ever separate each item of that from all the hearsay of the South Seas, all the Troano Manuscript, all the hundreds of things he'd found out and collected for his book?

From all Le Plongeon's talk to him, he felt he was in a way an heir to Le Plongeon's ideas and must also acknowledge that. So in the Lost Continent Of Mu, we find this attempt to cover the ground obliquely; on page 235 of that book:

> The late Dr. Augustus Le Plongeon and his wife Madame Alice D. Le Plongeon, were very dear friends of the writer.
> Before the death of Dr. Le Plongeon, he gave the writer his unpublished notes and translations for copy, so that what I say <u>about Yucatan</u> (italics mine, P.T.G.) comes principally from the result of Dr. Le Plongeon's 12 years among the ruins, much of which, however, I have corroborated by a personal examination.

I can see Churchey writing that in his handsome legible script, and sighing with relief that he had done more justice to old Le Plongeon than anyone else would have, and yet nicely saved his own face and not let himself down before these sceptical Yankees who demanded so much of him. I know **Churchey was no heir of Le Plongeon, whose notes and photos and materials were left with his widow, who wrote on Mu herself.**

Throughout the book, where some over enthusiastic impulse has obviously led him to endorse as personal knowledge an inference from other facts, and in his story of the tablets, one may see clearly the effect of his having started twice to make a romance of it all, and let his imagination legitimately run riot, luxuriating in fictional unrestraint and blank warrant.

236

He just couldn't let those Naacal tablets go. They were the whole introduction to his romance of Mu. Had he never thought of writing fiction, there'd have been no Naacal or other tablets. Had he been publishing in England, with the English Churchward family looking on, I don't think he'd have succumbed. But those tablets would wake up the world to his story of Mu, and anyway there were enough real evidences in his book that scientists couldn't overlook.

I have told of his total loss of memory about the St. Lawrence River skiff I gave him. Of other events in life, which he couldn't remember. Of his pitiable attempts to relate and rehearse the events of his steel experiences and experiments. All before the great debacle and shattering of his nerve.

Tout comprendre est tout pardonner. Churchey was old and miserable and bitter and a bit crabbed on the world at large. He was tired in many ways. The marvel is that he so courageously kept on with Mu, and with his efforts to get it published. That he did as well as he did, in the ways we are debating here.

That Naacal tablet matter must have appealed to him greatly, in the mood in which he was. I had shown him he couldn't in a serious work claim to have read a Mayan tablet, as he didn't know Mayan and others did. I had also warned him that the meagre heiroglyphic marks on a tablet someone had told him had something about the fall of Mu on it, (if anyone ever had, which is rather dubious, as he hadn't ever spoken of it in all our talks until he made it fiction, and agreed to drop that fable if he dropped the fiction end)couldn't possibly contain the vast amount of matter of a Troano Manuscript as large as a moderate-sized room. Grudgingly he had relinquished the Mayan tablet as a hot potato stuffed with visible T N T.

But he had "stumbled across" a reference in Le Plongeon's works to the Naacals: Page 199 of Queen Moo and the Egyptian Sphinx; Appendix:

> The verb Naacal means to be elevated, to be raised. It was the title adopted by the initiates among the Mayas * * * Transported to India, the word became corrupted in course of time to Naaca or Naga. The title was kept by the initiates who settled in the Dekkan and in Burmah.

Here was his chance. No one knew Naacal, the tongue of the initiates, and of the Nagas whose Empire was extinguished too many centuries ago to make them show up on Fifth Avenue New York or in newspaper offices with challenging gestures. Naacal tablets they would be. But could he, when he gave up the idea of fiction, part with his Naacal tablets? It seems he couldn't, though he had promised me he would.

Of course, as he didn't know how to read Mayan, he obviously couldn't read the language of the Mayans who were initiates. Was their tongue any different from their native speech because they had become initiates into religious mysteries and been termed Naacals? Churchey evidently didn't stop to consider that. Nobody knew a Naacal from a Communist or a Japanese beetle. A Naacal was a safe bet for his romance of Mu, and ought to be passably safe even if he shed the fiction. There was no one to suggest that Mayan was Mayan whether spoken by Mayan chiefs or Mayan initiates; or that if a Naacal had a special Mayan talk for himself and friends, any English philologist who could read that Naacal Mayan could surely read plain Mayan; which admittedly the Colonel couldn't.

In the Children of Mu Churchey, having launched the Naacal tablet story, and stood the gaff from it, and found his head bloody but unbowed, stood stoutly to his guns and fired a defiant broadside of Naacal in several places at a helpless reading public, (page 50 of Children of Mu e.g.):

    Color of Men's Skins....Let us go back 25,000 or 35,000 years and see what the old Naacals thought of it:
    The cause and causes which have been instrumental in causing the color of men's skins to change are various, but the principal cause has been unbalancing between the Life Force and the elementary compounds forming the skin. This unbalancing was the result of an over or an under stimulation of the glands which carry the Life Force in its secretions through the blood to the various parts of the body, including the skin..... (and so on for some 26 lines of print.)

This, says Churchey, is the best I can do to crack the hard Naacal nut * * the foregoing is an extract from the Naacal writings on the Origin of Life and What Life Is."

If I had shown that socalled translation of an ancient stone tablet to the Colonel Churchward I knew in his virile prime, he would have roared a gargantuan laugh and denounced it as absurd. The ancient heiroglyphs and cunieform and hieratic writing on stone or clay tablets contain no such modes of thought. They read like Le Plongeon's

Mayan chart of the Greek alphabet just shown in the diagrams compared: Al paa ta be ta kam ma.... Heavily break waters over plains cover earth etc. Can you imagine an ancient clay tablet debating in the abstract refined language of the Prince of Wales' tutor of the year 1855 the intricate thought of the "causes which have been instrumental in causing (!) the color of men's skins......by the unbalancing between the Life Force and the elementary compounds (!) which form the skin, and so forth ?

From long years of hearing Churchey's unique thoughts on kindred subjects, expressed in the same unique mode of thought, all I can say is, if that is "Naacal" language, then my old friend Churchey had been talking Naacal all his life unconsciously. Like Moliere's Bourgeois Gentilhomme who was astonished to learn he had been talking prose all his years. For never did a mode of thinking and theorizing and analysing so distinctly Churchwardian come under my vision until I read it some years ago in this "Naacal" explanation 35,000 years ago of what, however clear to those superior intellects, is still muddy to me the more I drink in their Naacal wisdom.

But as the Colonel read those tablets before he came to America when I was an infant, the supreme knowledge on skins didn't soak in at the time. For I have heard him speculate *at divers times diversely* on the color of men's skins as *due to* action of the atmosphere, of the sun's rays through a certain air, the rays reflected from certain rocks or underground deposits of minerals, and lastly in more mature years, that it was due to what the tribe ate in a certain geographically delimited area, which they inhabited. Why he never shot that unbalancing of the Life Force and other things at me when the kind old Naacals had left him their learned tablets forty years before telling him the mighty truth, I'll never know.

Of course there were no "Naacal" tablets, and if there ever had been, Churchey could no more read them than you or I, as he had admitted to me.

But this didn't prevent his works from selling extensively. The Lost Continent of Mu was followed in 1931 by The Children of Mu, in 1933 by The Sacred Symbols of Mu, and in 1934 by Cosmic Forces as they were Taught in Mu. He is said to have had hundreds of thousands of readers, and I know he made many disciples.

His works are well worth reading, and anyone who hasn't read them would do well to get a copy of The Lost Continent or The Children of Mu or the Sacred Symbols. Make a few allowances for what I have indicated here. Don't waste any time over the Naacal tablets. Accord old Le Plongeon the credit I have pointed out herein. Even hand Madame Alice Le Plongeon a little due her too. The beautiful picture of Prince Coh in war armor bodily in the Lost Continent of Mu is taken from Madame Alice's Queen Moo's Talisman, page 35, and the last illustration which marks finis to Churchward's first book, is taken from her description in the same work, p. xix: "representation of the Sun, in whose centre is an all-seeing eye within a triangle, from which depends a large tongue "(omitted)

Do not, in visioning Churchey's and your forefathers (gin the story's right) living in a golden age in Mu, use the Colonel's magnifying spectacles. Like those of the impoverished Spanish grandee, which showed him a skinny sparrow on his bare table as a plump turkey, Churchey's (made by those Naacal initiates in Burma) revealed the denizens of Mu as higher in culture, science, philosophic probing of the Universe, than any present-day descendants of these paragons.

No. What we know of man thousands of years ago in Egypt, Chaldea, India, and Israel and other places, displays him as a fellow of often lofty ideas but rather low in knowledge, prone to accept any crazy notions that came into his skull, priest-ridden, superstitious, cruel, crafty, and sadistic. All of which underlay the developing virtues which each century seem to augment in him.

It is known that the Mayans in Yucatan were good astronomers for their day, good agriculturists, good warriors. That they sacrificed thousands of human beings on the altars of their gods, and practiced haruspicy, the divination of events and the future by examining the entrails of beasts and men. They were just what you might expect from your studies of antiquity, from the knowledge you have that as you go back in time, you find man nearer and nearer to the savage and the beast, and to the child mentally.

But you will gain from the Colonel's fat volumes, besides many interesting hours, a mass of facts bearing on the question on which the Colonel spent forty years of research, which was first propounded by my venerable friend Dr. Le Plongeon: Does an examination of facts about the Mayans in Yucatan, of the Troano Manuscript and the Codex Cortesianus, with a comparison of identical cultures, manners, customs and mysteries in other ancient civilizations, indicate that all these nations came from a motherland of Mu, submerged by a cataclysm some 12,000 or more years ago?

You will, I think, decide with Churchward that Mu was in the Pacific, not the Atlantic, as Le Plongeon believed. What you will do about Atlantis I don't know. You may conclude that there is too much evidence of its previous existence to dismiss. You may decide that it is too much of a coincidence that both Mu in the Pacific, and Atlantis in the West Indies, both sank in a ghastly National debacle.

But I think you will end up with me, that the subject is worthy of serious and scrupulously careful research in the future. Especially as Le Plongeon and Churchward have blazoned the way, and started the ball with an array of facts that cannot be disregarded.

Both of these friends of mine firmly believed that he was but the opener of the battle, and that a future army would follow in his trail. Now that I have cut away from the Churchward volumes the stupid extraneous matter needlessly let creep into them, these works are open to the scientist to consult without the feeling that he is being "made a monkey of" with a lot of twaddle about Naacal tablets visible nowhere and readable by no one.

When The Lost Continent of Mu came out, I was immediately appealed to by men who knew Colonel Churchward and my relations with him all my life, for an authoritative expression upon the genuineness of his discoveries, and the truth of his claims.

In every instance but one I declined to make any comment at the moment. The exception was in Berlin in 1931, year of the publication of the second book, Children of Mu. My friend Dr. Wilhelm Cuno, former Chancellor of Germany, at luncheon at the Esplanade asked me about Colonel Churchward, whom he had met in America, and who was desirous of enlisting his backing for some explorations in Yucatan. To Geheimrath Cuno I told briefly the story of Churchward and Steel, Le Plongeon and Mu. I recommended his interesting himself in the subject, but under suitable conditions.

I did not wish to make any statement about Churchward and Mu. I felt that while I had introduced him to the Le Plongeons, and was the only person who knew the full truth about his work in the Mu matter, and about those tablets, I was likewise the last person to speak one word that might hurt the feelings of my old comrade, chum of my boyhood, my fishing partner, my fellow-victim in the Steel battle of the century.

He was old, much older than he admitted, and I hoped he would reach the hundred mark. For any shot at him to come from me would have been unthinkable.

I held no post of trust requiring me to pass

out judgment. I was Cincinnatus, not Justinian.

I knew old Fisherman Churchey couldn't tell his yarn without exaggerating his fish. It was in his blood. It had been so with his tie-plate, so with his Steel. But despite that, Churchey did get the biggest fish and the largest catches. His tie-plate was the best of all. His steel was superior and unmatched before or since. And I knew that, although he spoiled his remarkable work on Mu with trimmings, he had done the most and gone the furthest, in collating all the facts about Mu and the subject of the colonizing of all the civilizations of antiquity.

He felt that the American public demanded a tall story or didn't consider it worth the telling. I knew he had pondered so much on Mu that the wonder was he could tell where he got any of his data, much less allocate it all exactly,

How much had he and his brother Albert discussed and worked up? How much from those other Churchwards in the Pacific whom I have mentioned? I was aware he had drawn much from his travels in Asia and the South Seas, and that he was not a trained scientist with a fad for order and card-indexing his knowledge. His file was his brain, which swallowed all this food and turned it into Churchward thoughts and theories.

His wish to give credit to all is manifest in his books. His many references to hundreds of sources shows it. His constantly referring to Le Plongeon evinces a desire to recognize his debt to him, as much as he could without identifying his own contribution with that of a man he felt had been on the wrong Atlantis track.

As to the tablets, he had been planning a romance, with the tablets as a prologue. He had switched back to fact instead of fiction. He knew he ought to throw out the tablets, but he couldn't. In his prime he would have. But he was shattered in nerve and memory, he was but a shadow of the old Colonel of my youth. And he took the tablets along with him, instead of leaving them behind with the romantic imaginings and characters of his intended novel.

His Mu would have done even better without them than it did. It was the childish trimmings he added on, that drew the trimmings he received from some reviewers.

In outlining his life with its shocks, and his work on Mu, as I knew them and him; in showing how in his old age he let matters creep into the work which he shouldn't have; I do not wish to condone scientific inaccuracy. I stand four-square for scientific truth above all. But I plead guilty to showing the trend and the reasons as I have, not only for correction of the record, but also in extenuation of the errors, by analysing how they came into being.

I have held my tongue as long as I may, and in opening my mouth I must use my voice also to narrate all there is in palliation as in clarifying the facts. The old Colonel went to his "chamber in the silent halls of death" a couple of years ago, and I am now free to speak out without hurting him. If it can be done with added value to his works permanently, added weight to his reputation, it is clearly my duty to do so.

I feel that I do the old man much good and no harm in putting forth the truth. Others feel exactly the same as I. If Churchey himself could answer, I think he would feel so too. There are thousands of scholars, scientists, archaeologists, historians, here and abroad, who have cherished a too unjust opinion of Colonel Churchward as a charlatan in his story of Mu, and his minute details of the customs of Mu allegedly set forth in his Naacal tablets.

The truth does not harm anyone whose fame has been clouded by the absence of it. "The truth shall set you free." To know the career and character of Colonel Churchward and what he went through, to comprehend all that contributed to his success and to the breaking of his iron constitution and nerve; is to appraise justly all he did and to pardon his few errors.

Churchey in his old age remained the visionary, the dreamer, broken and pessimistic in all except this life-vision of the sunken Island of Mu. It is too much to expect that he would be able to filter fact from fancy in all particulars, as he did in most.

Always he had been the typical inventor whose despondency of today is matched by absurd exaggerated illusions tomorrow. Trusting and suspicious, confiding and sceptical, hopeless and over-elated, truthfully exact and wofully exaggerative by turns, by the shift of the hours, by the forces in which he was tossed about as a shipwrecked sailor in a maelstrom, by the subconscious struggles of the man to meet the attrition and onslaughts of environment.

Besides setting him straight before the world in the Mu matter, leaving what he actually contributed crystal-clear; I probably also do him an outweighing service in registering the true facts of the valuable work of Colonel Churchward in producing one of the great steels of all time. Pigeon-holed from the Government and largely from industry by business expediency, it remains still the same super-tensile-strong valuable giant of useful service, that it was when it triumphantly resisted all ballistic tests of the War and Navy departments, when it protected our sailors and marines on warships in the War, when it sturdily revolved in the gears of a million autos.

Since you cannot forever crush facts, I may be restoring its use to the world, which is free to make it now, the patents having expired.

A wreath on your grave, old Churchey! It includes some roses and bluebells from gardens bordering streams we fished time long past, some heather from Devon, even a few immortelles and a bit more laurel than you were allotted here. May it rest lightly there, and may you sleep soundly after all the strains and stresses which even the strength of your innate genius and geniality could not wholly withstand. If you dream perchance, as you believed, if you retrace the steps of your mundane years, may you be sitting in a St. Lawrence River skiff with a good guide and your old meerschaum, the fish coming to your skilful line as in the old days.

And if you chance to tell anyone there that it was a fifty pound muskallonge you just pulled in, I'm sure they'll forgive you, old Fisherman, and understand.

Vale, Colonel !

Taps.

www.ingramcontent.com/pod-product-compliance
Lightning Source LLC
Chambersburg PA
CBHW080323080526
44585CB00021B/2442